Hoein' the Short Rows

Hoein' the Short Rows

Edited by Francis Edward Abernethy

Publications of the Texas Folklore Society
Number XLVII

SOUTHERN METHODIST UNIVERSITY PRESS

First edition, 1987
Requests for permission to reproduce material from this work
should be sent to:
Permissions
Southern Methodist University Press
Box 415
Dallas, Texas 75275

Library of Congress Cataloging-in-Publication Data

Hoein' the Short Rows.

(Publications of the Texas Folklore Society; 47)
Includes index.
1. Folklore—Texas. 2. Texas—Social life and
customs. I. Abernethy, Francis Edward. II. Series:
Publications of the Texas Folklore Society; no. 47.
GRI.T4 no. 47   390 s   87-9756
[GRI 10.T5]   [398'.09764]
ISBN 0-87074-256-6

DESIGNED BY *Whitehead & Whitehead*

The Texas Folklore Society dedicates its forty-seventh volume,
Hoein' the Short Rows, to
Martha Emmons

Martha Emmons, then a history teacher at Taylor High School, was sent her copy of *Legends of Texas* (PTFS III, 1924) and was enrolled as a member of the Texas Folklore Society by Ethel Burch, Frank Dobie's secretary, on June 3, 1924. She was invited to add to the Texas legends that Dobie was then collecting and presented her first paper, "Folk-lore of Williamson County," on May 9, 1925, at the Austin meeting. She published her first paper, "Confidences from Old Nacogdoches," in *Foller de*

Drinkin' Gou'd (PTFS VII) in 1928. The 1932 volume, *Tone the Bell Easy* (PTFS X), took its title from her article, "Dyin' Easy." Miss Martha was the program chairman for the April 21–22, 1933, meeting at Baylor University, for which she was highly commended by Dobie, and subsequently she ascended the political ladder to become president of the Society in 1935–36. Thirty-five years later in 1970 she was again elected to that office.

For sixty-four years Martha Emmons has served and instructed and entertained the Society. She has guarded its virtue with staunch Baptist morality and has cherished its children with Christian love. The Texas Folklore Society and all of its members abundantly return that love to Miss Martha and thank her for the richness of the many years she has given us.

CONTENTS

PREFACE

*In which the editor spins a long tale
in defense of a short title
and is ultimately rescued by
Mody Boatright.*

I NEVER did like to hoe, and when I was staying on the farm with my grandparents I didn't have to hoe much anyhow, being my granddad's own sweet child. Even as a small boy I had my own hoe, however, which had a three-foot handle and about two inches of blade left, and I went to the cotton fields on inclination or when everybody else was there.

Walking from the house to the cotton field was about a quarter of a mile alongside a downhill cowpath that had washed out a foot deep in places. Granddad always pointed out that in this very cow trail was where I should get if I ever saw a cyclone headed my way and couldn't make it back to the dugout. Many a cowboy had saved his life, he said, by scrooching down in a washed-out cow or buffalo trail. Even then, one cowboy had his pocketknife and watch completely sucked out of his pockets when the cyclone passed over him. Another poor son lost his boots and his britches. I often pondered the effect of such a phenomenon on a boy who wore only overalls. It was enough to make one ever wátchful for cyclones out on those Texas plains.

Jack and Pal, brother dogs that caught and swallowed biscuits in one fell gulp, always went with us to the field. They would range far out ahead, probing the Johnson grass along the fence lines for rabbits. Failing that, they would make a few sallies down the cotton rows which also generally proved unproductive. After which they would hunt the shade and would conclude their odyssey lying in a freshly hoed cotton row, as close to the water jug as was allowable. Water jugs were one-gallon glass jugs wrapped in tow sack that had been sewed up with binder twine. The wrapped jug was dipped in the horse trough on the way to the field, and the only humidity in that part of the Texas Panhandle was what radiated from the water jug, and it was soaked up in a millisecond by brothers Jack and Pal and attendant gnats.

Hoeing in the morning was easier than hoeing during the heat of the afternoon, but mornings were long enough. The beautiful sight to see was the open door to the cottonseed shed up at the house. That was the signal for the hands to come in to dinner. We napped on the porch after dinner with the dogs and the cats and the summer gnats that were eternally and mystically drawn to the underside of a straw-hat brim. Afternoon hoeing was relieved only by the thought that when it was over we could go to the Washita that ran below the fields and bathe and cool off. I exaggerate when I say the Washita "ran." During the dry Thirties it "stood" in small pools of bed sand. But it was still a sweet balm to ease the pain from the day's heat and dust.

I admire good hoe hands and have always been fascinated by the skill and seeming ease of the operation as they move easily along the rows chopping with clean, effortless strokes that go "chiu-chiu-chiu." Dad, who is in his mid-eighties, can still hoe a garden row quicker, cleaner, and neater than anybody I teach English with. He attributes his expertise to keeping his hoe sharp and not allowing dirt to cake up on it and advises that I do the same. I'm sure those are factors in good hoeing and are work habits I would cultivate more assiduously, were I a better son.

This cotton patch of which I speak—and which still stands hot and dusty in the everyoung eye of my mind—had an angle on one side of it, caused by a shallow draw along its margin. The draw grew lamb's-quarter which Grandmother picked and we ate, and it also produced, one vivid time, a huge snake which she vigorously cut into links with a hoe that was sharp and clean enough to shave with. The draw was another place where I moved with careful attention to the details of my surroundings, conscious of dangers that lurked in addition to those that hovered.

The draw, besides furnishing us with lamb's-quarter and great hissing and rattling snakes, angled the last cotton rows down to several diminishing rows, each one shorter than the last. If there was ever any pleasure in hoeing, it was in these final short rows soon hoed rather than the first ones that in the high heat of the day seemed to stretch into shimmering eternity.

And that's what this 1987 anthology of Texas folklore is and why it is so named. It is a series of short rows, easily and pleasantly hoed, promising a rich crop as a reward for the readers' labors. These are the best of the Society's papers over the past two years, with a sprinkling of extras.

I've long had problems with titles for PTFS miscellanies. Some book buyers thought *Paisanos* was a book about road-runners, *T for Texas* was a collection of country music, and *Sonovagun Stew* was a cookbook. Relying on these former mis-conceptions, Al Lowman suggested the title *Hoein' the Short Rows*, on the basis that we could make some sales of this volume to persons looking for a book on agriculture. If so, I hope that their initial disappointment will be tempered and surprised by the wealth of readable, informative, and enjoy-able essays contained herein.

I myself was surprised by some of the inclusions—and I refer specifically to the articles on "folk poetry." I had already struggled with the "folk poetry" concept. Cowboy "folk po-etry" got a lot of mileage after the Elko Cowboy Poetry Gath-ering of 1985, and I went so far as to buy the book that came out of that meeting. But I had trouble getting it through my head that what they were producing was either "poetry" or "folk." I try not to be a literary snob, but much of what I've encountered under the label of folk poetry has been doggerel. Some of it achieved the status of verse. I encountered very little poetry. And I never was able to justify it according to the usual characteristics of folklore—oral, traditional, variational, anonymous, formularized, etc. Most of it hasn't circulated among the folk long enough to be tested for survival in the world of folklore. Much of the verse, however, is vigorous, picturesque, sharply descriptive, and fun to read, more so than some modern art verse I encounter. Rough though some of it might be, it follows the conventional verse forms and the well-used rhyming and rhythmical patterns. And much of it deals with traditional folkways and philosophies. The poet or versifier is writing to his peers, those in his culture circle, who feel as he does about the subject of the verse. And if one can accept washpots and turning plows in the front yard as folk art, then logically he should accept a cowboy's anapestic te-trameter couplets as folk poetry. I long ago accepted "Straw-berry Roan"; I now accept this volume's collections of folk poetry and will continue attempting to broaden my folklore horizons.

I have for fifteen years been indebted to good folklore writers, both amateur and professional, within the Society and lingering on the fringes. I thank the contributors to *Short Rows* for their time and effort and for their continuing interest in the folklore that is a part of their lives. The Society has long been the beneficiary of folklore amateurs, and much of its richest material has come from folks who simply relate the folklore in their own lives and the lives of their families. The previous editors of the PTFS took special care for these people and were ever ready to come to their defense when they came under attack by unsympathetic professionals. I would like to conclude this preface with a defense that Mody Boatright jotted down sometime during the 1960s.

I found this satirical fragment by Mody in one of his files after the TFS records had been transferred to Nacogdoches. It was typed but it looked like a first copy. The title was "Com-ments on Richard Dorson's 'Bogies of American Folklore,'" and it was a subtly sarcastic response to Dorson's continued riding of his "fakelore" hobby horse. My conjecture is that Mody dashed it off in a fit of aggravation at Dorson but never had occasion to either present it or publish it. Ernest Speck said that Mody once told him that if he heard Dorson say "fakelore" one more time he was going to retch, wherever he might happen to be at the time. Mody's mock-serious "Comments" are sentiments he and I share, and I share them with you.

Comments on Richard Dorson's "Bogies
of American Folklore"
—By Mody C. Boatright

Every organization, every group with a community of interest, however tenuous that interest may be, must have bogies; for without bogies to compel continuous self-examination, definition, and redefinition, complacency and ultimate loss of purpose may be expected.

So every group needs its bogie hunters whose function is to haul the bogies into the court of group opinion, where their orthodoxy or heterodoxy may be debated, and where some consensus may be reached—a consensus that will last only until new bogies arise, or until the old ones attempt a new infiltration.

Believing then, as I do, in the value of what Dorson has done, I wish to join him by presenting a couple of bogies of my own.

BOGIE NO. 1B (B is for Boatright). Amateurism is to be combatted on all fronts. This proposition has many corollaries, three of which I shall state.

Col. No. 1. Lore collected and written down by amateurs may not be used by professionals. Let us say there is a man who remembers having been taken to a faith-healer at the age of seven to have his warts removed. If he is interviewed by a professional, he becomes an informant, and the information elicited from him is valid. But if of his own accord he writes and publishes an account of the event as he remembers it, the information is invalid.

Col. No. 2. The folklorist must not write for a general audience, because a general audience will contain more amateurs than professionals. A simple and widely used device for limiting the audience to professionals is to write in a style that nobody else will read.

Col. No. 3. All amateurs should be expelled from the folklore societies, particularly from the American Folklore Society, and the dues of the professionals should be increased to the figure necessary for the Society to carry on in the manner to which it has become accustomed.

BOGIE NO. 2B. Folklore is a science, the techniques of which have already been perfected, largely by Europeans.

Col. No. 1. This technique consists of abstracting the elements of folklore (somehow analogous to neutrons, photons, electrons, and the like) and treating them as independent entities.

Col. No. 2. All considerations, even by implication, of social or esthetic value, are to be rigidly excluded.

Col. No. 3. Satisfactory scholarly results have been obtained when the material has been analyzed and the proper index and type numbers have been assigned. The value of the study will be enhanced if a plausible provenience can be conjectured.

Col. No. 4. Since type and index numbers presently exist only for prose narrative, the great task before us, overshadowing all others, is the compilation of indices for ballad and song, music, games, beliefs, riddles, proverbs, customs, and artifacts.

It's always heartwarming when Mody drops in on a visit.

FRANCIS EDWARD ABERNETHY
Stephen F. Austin State University
Nacogdoches, Texas
March 1987

JOYCE GIBSON ROACH

A High Toned Woman

In a song made popular by
Tennessee Ernie Ford, the male in "Sixteen Tons" complains
that, among other troubles, "ain't no high toned woman
make me walk the line." From one hardworking man's point
of view, high toned women should be avoided. Such a woman
might want to improve upon or change the naturalness of a
man who could load sixteen tons. In contrast, and in words
from a modern translation of Old Testament sentiment, a
good woman of Jack County was laid to rest with these words,
"She is a worthy woman, high toned, more valuable than
rubies and her husband and family rise up and call her blessed."
Who then was this creature, this High Toned Woman, feared
and suspected by some, venerated and adored by others? Did
she really exist? And when? Can we take her dimensions, test
her worthiness, name her parts, examine her, proclaim her
riches? And how does the High Toned Woman fit into the
great chain of being and on the ladder of other female types—
mothers, others, doormats, schoolmarms, Lesbians, Ama-
zons, and the liberated who can "bring home the bacon, fry it
up in the pan, and never ever let you forget you're a man"?
Where do we find her, how do we identify her, rescue her, and
name a movement after her? Can we actually find one to call
by name and to bestow upon her the label *folk heroine?* To
answer all these deep, deep questions "which lie too deep for
tears," is the purpose of this paper. And in view of the past
Sesquicentennial year of 1986, when women were hung on
the line naked for all the world to see and were the subject of

papers, seminars, university courses, discussion groups, town meetings, banking services, support shelters, counseling sessions, half-way houses, hospital facilities, and even books, it is my purpose to take one long, last look at a type which has, up to now, been completely and thoroughly neglected and, by so doing, to lay completely to rest one more female type on the "sunny slopes of long ago."

Who or what were High Toned Women? They were those women in every small community who counted themselves as the authorities in matters both temporal and spiritual, but mostly spiritual. They could organize, direct, conduct, and orchestrate feminine matters; could fine tune, refine, regulate, and monopolize the female psyche; and could judge, draw, and quarter unworthy opponents. They were looked up to, respected, and emulated for their clear judgment, their unerring fortitude, their dogged pursuit of truth as they saw it, their unflagging dedication to showing the rest of us how to live. They were the nearest thing a community had to folk heroines, and they strutted in a hen yard just big enough to accommodate them.

High Toned Women were found in rural communities where little contact and influence from the outside world was possible, or else there was just enough contact to get matters all mixed up and to pick out the most glaring faults of the civilized city and cast them in country molds. Churches served as the community clubhouses, so to speak, and were the meeting grounds several times a week for not only High Toned Women but every other variety. Opportunities were many to practice the female arts in Sunday School, which in some churches was an all-female group, Sunday morning worship, Training Union, Sunday evening services, Wednesday evening prayer meeting, women's missionary groups, choir practice, weddings, funerals, Bible study, and class socials.

Although High Toned Women might be viewed anywhere in the community from the post office to the bank to any store around the square, they were on display in all their glory at church. I fellowshipped with the Baptists, but Methodists, Pentecostals, Churches of Christ, and Presbyterians had choice entries in the High Toned category too. They scratched and clucked in their own yards and only rarely got in each other's way, sometimes at a revival. Usually there were no more than three to any given territory. It seemed to be the rule, however, that whatever denomination held a revival, the visiting High Toned Women yielded to the women in the presiding church.

Within the church, High Toned Women were most obvious in the choir, usually in the front row in the soprano section. Sometimes a fine alto got in on the ladder, but altos sat behind the sopranos; therefore the front-row soprano had the upper hand. At times, deep emotion, or perhaps contrition, during the closing hymn played upon the face of a High Toned Woman as the words (or perhaps the sound of her own splendid voice) moved her to shake her head, close her eyes, take out her handkerchief, let her voice break (for a moment only and never long enough to cause her to lose control of her pitch), and gasp for a moment. Did anyone come forward? Ah well, perhaps another verse. High Toned Women paid no attention to the choir director, but rather let the spirit, through them, lead the choir, the preacher, and the entire flock into ten more verses. High Toned Women always knew best the mood and disposition of the Holy Spirit. I have often wondered if the custom of the "long call" was instituted by a High Toned soprano and not by any pleading preacher.

Personally, I learned early to take the cue from the choir. The long call was unnecessary. I plunged down the aisle at every opportunity at every revival, every church, and gave my heart to whatever cause was pending—missionary work at the stop sign at the edge of town, praying on the street, singing on the curb, teaching on the sidewalk, persuading by the wayside. Religiously, I've been on more street corners than the *Dallas Times Herald*. It became obvious and alarming to my family that by the time I was twelve, I was a High-Toned-

Woman-In-Training—a docent in the museum of rural high society.

It was not in the choir, however, that High Toned Women worked the hardest. It was in the congregation on Sunday mornings and "amongst" the masses at revival. Although there were some variations on the grand theme, almost all High Toned Women were large and fleshy women, wore corsets, had hour-glass figures, donned hats and gloves for all religious occasions, and carried black purses with strap handles. When they came into the aisles from the back of the church or arbor, their entrance reminded of great ships at sea as they turned their bows into the wind. Sailing relentlessly on to the front with their summer-weight dresses rippling and flapping like sails in their own breeze, we felt the platform tremble and the planks of the benches moan as their well-staved masts groaned and creaked against the rigging of their underwear.

It was in the church aisles that the real power of a High Toned Woman was sometimes wielded. When the invincible ironsides turned her guns on sin and sinners who ought to be at the altar, the smoke billowed, the air hung heavy with the smell of fire and brimstone, and it seemed indeed that "the earth did shake and the veil of the temple was rent in twain," as a High Toned Woman wrestled during the long call with the devil in the soul of some misguided youth or hardened husband. And no one could keep his head bowed and his eyes closed *too*, for we all wanted to witness the power of a tongue in flames as the High Toned Woman pleaded, exhorted, and called down God Almighty and a few angels to assist her in bringing a lost soul home. Her voice intoned, "Oh, sinner, if just one soul like you is saved tonight, the angels in heaven weep." That was probably no exaggeration. Meanwhile, in the choir another High Toned Woman jumped into another verse of "Almost Persuaded" to assure her sister of a little more time with the stubborn, hardheaded, nasty little sinful son-of-a-saint.

There may have been High Toned Women in cities. We

often speculated that there might be some in Dallas, but we never knew for sure. We knew Fort Worth was a big town, but still a country town and their ways were not the stranger's ways. But Dallas! Dallas was such a dangerous place and we didn't go—hardly ever. All the women there were Quality, which is not the same as High Toned or the same as Choice or Prime. I had Quality explained to me once in Dallas, by my grandmother. Mama Hartman took me once, when I was a small girl, inside the very walls of Neiman-Marcus. We kept to the sides of the store, never venturing into the aisles except to get to another wall. She allowed me to look swiftly at whatever goods were on eye level, but she kept a firm grip on my hand. The ladies who were shopping paid no attention to us, and so I got to look at them all I wanted. What I saw was Quality.

"We are going to hunt the bathroom."

"But, Mama, you told me never to go to the bathroom in a strange house and never, never in a department store 'cause you never knew who'd been usin' the pot. You said, if you were desperate, never to sit on the seat—never—but to hunker above it. And then when you do go, it leaves the seat all wet all over it and you either have to clean up or else not let anybody see you leave because they'd know you were the one who did it on the seat. You said it was better to hold in no matter what; and to always go to the bathroom the last thing before you left the house. Mama, I don't need to use Neiman-Marcus' bathroom." I was pulling back now and whispering so she wouldn't shush me.

"I know all that, Joyce Ann." Now she was whispering so I wouldn't shush her. There was enough rush of noisy air coming from our mouths to have launched a hot air balloon. "I want you to see something."

We pushed open the door and there was only one Quality woman in the place. She was washing her hands and tucking her hair up. She licked one finger and pushed up her eyebrow. Then she licked another finger and pushed up the other one. Anyone could tell that she was a good, clean woman since she didn't lick the same finger to do the other brow. She was certainly a lesson in Quality. Watching Quality at her toilette was not, however, what Mama had in mind. When the lady left, after giving a good tug to her girdle, we went to the first booth. The toilet seat was dry! We made every stall, eight of them, and—they were all dry!

Mama said, "See, Joyce Ann." I shook my head in amazement and agreement, but never till the day she died did I ever have the courage to ask an explanation about the dry toilet seats. The only logical conclusion was that Quality women took a better aim.

Being a High Toned Woman constituted a career of sorts for country women. The career offered many opportunities, good working conditions, selected hours, and executive positions only, but the pay was poor and chances for advancement were limited. After woman's oldest profession, and woman's second-oldest profession of motherhood, being a High Toned Woman might qualify as woman's third-oldest profession.

There was one rare opportunity for a High Toned Woman to advance in the world, unlike women in the first two professions. She could become a missionary. It seemed in my child's mind that every missionary I ever met was female and High Toned. That truth, of course, did not everywhere abound, but we all live by our own assumptions, and for all I knew, to be female was a requirement to being a missionary. What little we knew of geography or the larger world, we knew from mission study. God called upon missionaries and us to feed the hungry and to clothe the naked. I thought the African people needed our kind of food—corn bread and red beans, chicken fried steak, such as that—and I didn't worry about their getting it because good money went regularly to the mission fund and probably some good missionary prepared it herself around a cozy campfire in the jungle. (Another assumption was that Africans were the only ones who needed missionaries, and that they along with Tarzan and Cheetah had about all the bases covered.) But I could see how the missionaries *needed* help with the clothes. It was a long time, and only after repeated trips to the forbidden *National Geographic*, that I realized that the heathen Africans preferred nakedness and the missionaries preferred to have them cover their nakedness. The logic was clear. You couldn't have naked, brown humans running around disrobed in front of a High Toned Woman. I nearly wept when the truth sank in. Clothing the naturally naked was the high aim of the missionary movement before 1950. Such a work! To be able to gather barrels of clothes so that all Africans, every last naked one of them, might sweat, itch, and pull at tight underwear as I did was worthy of my best efforts. I could help civilize and robe them in a fashion worthy to be presented at the throne of God. I wanted to see every last God's one of them cinched, girded about the loins, trussed up, and covered with Fruit of the Loom, not with merely a fig leaf. Putting clothes on Adam and Eve was almost the first civilized act of God when the pair brought sin and civilization upon themselves, and I intended to make it my life's work by way of the U.S. mail. Wisdom was a long, long time in coming, and if in my mind I had to undress as many Africans as I had sworn to clothe, the job would not have been too great.

If it seems that High Toned Women were found consorting in merely busy business of predominantly religious affairs, it should be pointed out that the same women had a goodness about them unequalled in any period in history. These same women were the ones trusted to hold a dying child, called upon to console a widow, asked to bear sad news in a telegram which no woman should have to read from paper, relied upon to prepare graves, and honored for remembering all the proper rituals of the heart which have never been written down. If they were the authorities in matters of living, they were also the ones enduring enough to accompany us to the edge of the grave and to bring us back again to the land of the living, drawing us after them in footsteps plainly visible. Trained psychologists and psychiatrists would only wonder at the wisdom, the deftness in dealing with the human condition, the splendid appropriateness of their gestures and their words. The professionals should reach back in time and call them "sister."

But there is more: gifts of food, little surprises for the children they knew, gifts for acquaintances; they were peacemakers in family and community. The positive force which emanated from High Toned Women made many of them eligible for sainthood.

I do believe that the clan, High Toned, is universal and occurs in all civilizations from pagan to Christian, from Africa to South America, from Siberia to Australia, and represents a kind of feminine category peculiar to every nationality on earth. Somebody ought to fund a salary and give a professorship, free research assistants, and living accommodations to any writer who would hunt and write about the High Toned Woman. (They did all that for James A. Michener and he didn't even find out that there was such a creature in this incomparable state.)

The status and importance of High Toned Women were probably felt only in female domains. Males, as far as I could tell, paid no attention to them unless perhaps a preacher had to deal with them from time to time. There does not appear to be a related category known as High Toned Men, for instance. No one questioned a woman's role in male relationships either. It was usually a woman-to-woman thing. How women kept house may have been of some interest, but how they performed in the bedroom was a question peculiar only to 1970 and after, and by then High Toned Women were all gone. Most men probably felt like Ernie Ford, knowing that no High Toned Woman would make them walk the line— maybe.

The decline of High Toned Women began with World War II when women went to work and opened up a whole new classification of types. Radio, which brought the voices of the nation and the world into the living room, did no favor for High Toned Women. Movies occasionally captured one or two on film, but High Toned Women were always featured in supporting roles, which is, perhaps, what High Toned Women did best—support. Movies made of them merely Busy Bodies.

The Andy Hardy series comes to mind. Aunt Bee in the Andy Griffin television series approached High Toned, but fell short, too. It could be that Schick centers took up High Toned Women's work, and Dear Abby is as close a confidant as modern women can find. Barbara Walters asks questions that real High Toned Women avoided at all costs. When there is no need, High Toned Women, or any other institutions of folklore, pass away, and new forms of popular culture rise to fill the gap. I'm not so sure they have been replaced with "something of value."

I shall gladly help bury the High Toned Woman with tenderness, care, and sweet remembrance, but let no one say that I helped dig her grave. Do not forget the type. Go to some exotic, strange, remote, primitive, backward, rural, timeless place, if you can find it, and you will still find the High Toned Woman. She may not speak your language, but you will know her when you see her. If you would, perhaps, care to form a club, please meet me later. I am already the president, and so you need not apply for that job. And just as soon as I can get my corset laced and my hymnbook out, we shall stand outside on the corner and sing the anthem of High Toned Women, always done as a solo, "The Ninety and Nine," the last verse of which goes:

> And all through the mountains thunder riven
> And up from the rocky steep
> There arose a glad cry from the gates of heaven
> Rejoice I have found my sheep
> And the angels echoed around the throne
> Rejoice for the Lord brings back his own.
> Rejoice for the Lord brings back his own.

St. Louis Southwestern (Cotton Belt) engine 801. The engineer and
head brakeman are leaning out of the cab. This photo was taken in
Texarkana by R. S. Plummer. *From the John B. Charles Collection.*

CHARLIE ODEN

The Lingo of the Espee

RAILROAD people have enjoyed their own lingo over a sesquicentennial period of time and from sea to shining sea. The employees of the Southern Pacific, the Espee, use much of the jargon used on the other American railroad lines, but they have a lot of lingo that is their own. The following sample of the lingo of the Espee is both general and particular. It is but a sample of a jargon so large that it is almost a language in itself. During my more than forty years on the Southern Pacific's Dallas and San Antonio divisions, this lingo was my "first language" in which I both thought and communicated with others in the work of moving trains, beginning as a telegrapher-clerk and retiring as a chief train dispatcher.

Espee management contributed to the lingo. Beginning in the early 1920s and continuing for about sixty years, the Southern Pacific applied the term "Sunset Lines" to itself. Its logo was a circle within a circle with a horizontal connecting bar, and within the smaller circle was a railroad track running into a setting sun. The name "Sunset Limited" was given to trains one and two, both of which ran between Los Angeles and New Orleans with close connections from both terminals. This southern, all-weather route was touted as the "Sunset Route." The "Sunset" idea was born in San Antonio. In the early 1920s, during a time of austerity and cutbacks on the Southern Pacific, a young clerk named Allen was being paid to keep the cash accounts and was a day behind in his work when one of his bosses walked in and found him expressing his artistic skills on the Company's time and with the Company's materials. The boss saw Allen's desk covered with a day's unposted postings and a drawing of railroad tracks running into the setting sun, captioned SUNSET ROUTE. He fired the young man on the spot and told him to return the next day for his pay. Meanwhile, an Officer's Special from California arrived on an inspection tour. Mr. Henry Pierce, a capitalist from Boston and an investor in the Espee, was with the Special and happened to walk by ex-employee Allen's desk, saw the picture, and liked it. When Allen reported for his pay, he found that he had not been fired, that Mr. Pierce thought him quite an artist, and that he was a hero instead of a heel. Later, a side track near Marathon, Texas, was named Tesnus, which is Sunset spelled backward.

By and large, railroad jargon originates with the track, mechanical, and operating personnel. The track between Austin and Llano, now owned by the City of Austin, was originally a narrow gauge named The Austin and Northwestern. Between the time it was the A & NW and its purchase by Austin City, it was owned by Southern Pacific and referred to as the "Windy." The track between Victoria and Port Lavaca is the "Salty," and when cars arrive in Victoria enroute to Port Lavaca, or when there is switching to be done at Port Lavaca, Victoria calls a "Salty," that is, a train and engine crew, to handle a Port Lavaca turn, "turn" meaning round trip from one station to another and back. The 184 miles between Hearne and East Yard (the freight yard in San Antonio) is the "Dalsa" (Dallas—San Antonio cut off). Other railroads have been given pet names. The I & GN (International and Great Northern, now Union Pacific) is "The Jenny" and the Santa Fe is "John Santa Fe."

In addition to nicknaming portions of the railroad, the equipment was also given pet names, an engine being an "enjine," or in the case of a steam engine, a "kettle" or a "pot," and when in yard service, the "yard goat." The caboose is the "hack," the "crummy," or the "crumbox." Crews used to sleep and cook in their cabooses at away-from-home tie-up points. Those little red and green lights that one sees on the back of a

Southern Pacific Transportation Company logo.

caboose are "markers" because they mark the end of the train. Those electric lanterns which you see in the hands of train-men who are using them for hand signals took the place of the "hayburners," the company-issued kerosene lanterns. They are ten inches high and, with the bail extended, reach fifteen inches. The bottom is a small kerosene container with a wick extending up to the burner. The glass chimney is four inches high and three and one half inches in diameter. The top is a cap with holes in the perimeter to allow some, but not too much, draft. A wire guard protects the unit. Though these lanterns were issued for signaling, most men furnished their own electric lanterns, saying that the only thing the company issue was good for was setting fire to hay, hence, "hayburner." Refrigerator cars are "drippers," cattle cars in their time were "cow crates," gondolas are "gons," and ordinary boxcars are sometimes referred to as "car boxes."

From earliest times some sort of safety protection was needed where railroad tracks crossed. The need was met with interlockings. Early interlocking plants gave control of switches, derails, and signals to a person positioned in a tower who could watch and coordinate movements by means of lev-ers in the tower. Early plants connected the levers with de-rails, switches, and signals by means of steel rods, and re-quired brawny boys to line up the plant for a movement. Even after the advent of electrically powered plants, the manual plants were still called "armstrongs."

Towermen were usually telegraphers. The telegraph was used for certain communications up through World War II. It was used for "fall back" train-order transmissions when the telephones failed, and a reasonable skill in telegraphy was therefore a qualification that a train-order operator-towerman-clerk and a train dispatcher had to have. Some old-time conductors addressed the circa 1940 telegrapher-towerman-clerk as a "brass pounder," but that good name has disappeared. Naturally telegraphers had a little lingo of their own when using the wire. The business of the dispatcher, "di" or "ds," had priority on the wire, and when a telegrapher had a train coming at an on-line station to be cleared with orders, he could break any transmission with "bk, 9 di" and sign his call letters, say "FN" for Flatonia. Likewise, the dispatcher, needing Giddings for an order, would break the transmission with "bk, 9, US DS." The telegrapher would "clear" the train (get di's authority) and put the orders in a clothes-pin-type fastener on a bamboo hoop and "hand up" to both the head end and the caboose. The "bk" means break, and right today in 1987, an old telegrapher may, on being surprised at something said, interrupt with "BK! What did you say?" Men from other crafts were always amused at the telegraphers' verbalizing the morse code this way. The "9" means train order business, "25" means "I am busy," "73" means "regards" or "best wishes" and closes a conversation or a short joint transmission session with another telegrapher. Swearing was done with letters, i.e., Dm, or G.d., or g.t.h., etc.

Working positions on the Espee were also referred to in jargon. The train dispatcher is the "train delayer." Engineers are "hogheads," head brakemen are "head men" or "head shacks," and the rear brakeman is the "flag." He is the "flag" because when a train stops between stations, it is his responsibility to go back toward whence the train came, carrying fusees and "guns" (torpedoes) and a red flag by day (a red lantern by night) so as to intercept and stop any train following. The "skipper," or "brains," is the conductor who carries the "bills," the letter-size documents which accompany each car in the train and carry the information pertinent to that car: its initial, number, classification, origin, destination, lading, etc. He is in charge of the train and is responsible for its proper operation with the exception that the hoghead is responsible for the engine and some other matters over which the skipper has no real control. The yardmaster is the "yardboss"; the yard clerk who works in the yard is "catching numbers" and is the "mudhop." Car repairmen inspect the cars of inbound and outbound trains, making minor repairs or "bad ordering" any cars which should not go, but which should be placed to the "rip track" for repairs. These men are "car knockers."

Forty years on a railroad is long enough to witness the birth process of a nickname and the evolution of another. In the 1950s, a young man named Fred Ryberg "hired out" in train service and was later promoted to trainmaster in South Texas. Evidently someone's tang got tungled up when speaking Fred's name, and it came out "Fried Redbird." That was so good that word of it even reached that Mecca of Southern Pacific, the general office in San Francisco, in record time, and even those people enjoyed it. Fortunately, Fred's disposition also allowed him to enjoy it. Fred was such an officer as to be liked and respected by the men, and when the company named the fruit and vegetable train originating on his district the RGV (Rio Grande Valley), it was soon dubbed the "Ryberg Green Vegetables."

The evolution happened to the nickname "Bearcage." When a high-ranking operating officer is assigned a private car like the *Houston,* the car is referred to as the "Bearcage," and not without reason. Because of the vast territory encompassed by the San Antonio division after it absorbed the Dallas Division and most of the Victoria Division, the superintendent was assigned the *Houston* and used it to ride in when making division inspections. The car served as the Bearcage for about three superintendents, over a span of about fifteen or so years. Then one day, a thirty-year-old California aristocrat with Harvard Business School training was

Southern Pacific engine 922. This engine was typical SP freight power between Houston and Ennis as well as between Houston and El Paso and would be considered as "heavy" power. The photo was taken in Ennis by Ford Curry. *From the William J. Neill Collection.*

given the superintendency. We felt like second-class citizens around him. All through the years, when the private car was to move from San Antonio, the yardboss would call and tell the chief dispatcher, "We're adding the Bearcage on the rear end of the Bullet." Then one day about a year after we had inherited the young superintendent, I was talking by phone to the man in charge of the yard who remarked during the conversation, "The Bullet will be ready when we get the School Bus on him." "What school bus, Smokey?" Brief silence. "The business car *Houston.*" The young superintendent was reassigned to a lobbying job later on.

Trains were named. Trains No. 1 and No. 2, the Sunset Limiteds, were also called "The Ace" and "The Deuce." Between the years 1936 and 1956, Trains No. 13 and No. 14, the Sunbeams, operated between Houston and Dallas (265 miles in 265 minutes!) with streamlined engines and equipment, but for some strange reason, they never received names. The engines were sheathed in sheet metal to streamline them, and they looked to anyone watching their approach like colorful red-orange towers rushing along in long skirts. The banner train, the Blue Streak Merchandise, operated from East St. Louis to Los Angeles with piggybacks and automobile parts and ran at an authorized speed of 70 MPH with preference over all trains except Amtrak. And when we thought we could get by with it, we put the "Deuce" in the "hole" (siding) for him. This expedited schedule was known as "Old Blue" or just "Blue."

The terms of everyday operations are many and expressive. Freight trains must "clear" (be in the siding) before the scheduled time of first-class trains. Thus, the crew members of a freight train running from Houston to San Antonio must watch the time of the "Deuce." If their train is passing Flatonia at 5:40 A.M. and No. 2 is due out of Luling at 6:20 A.M., they have forty minutes in which to run to Luling and put their train in the clear. If they are passing Flatonia about 5:55 A.M., they will have only twenty-five minutes to make it, and if they do, it will be on "close time," and they will have just "scratched" Luling for the "Deuce." To be "in town" is to be at your destination. "Carrying the Green" refers to sections of schedules. Before the practice began of operating all freights as extras, a dispatcher would run two or more sections of a schedule when he knew that there was enough tonnage available to run two or more trains during the time when the specific schedule was available. For example, the Hearne dispatcher would run the first train to Houston as First 342 instead of No. 342.

Where a territory is protected by block signals, the track is divided into "blocks" by circuits, and signals are placed at each end of the block. During the time that a train is in a block, the signals at each end display red to any approaching train, and in this way countless collisions have been avoided. The members of a crew running a train watch the block signals, and when they see the "High Green," they know that the block they are about to enter is unoccupied. Standing in the cab, one can listen to the fireman call the signals to the engineer, "Green in the Valley," and the engineer's response, "Green in the Valley." A little later it may be "Yellow on the Hill," with the response "Yellow on the Hill." When they see a green over yellow, they know that the immediate block is clear, and something is in the next block. It is at this point that a passenger train engineer must begin slowing his train, and it is this circumstance that is referred to as "being yellow blocked," being delayed by caution signals set by a train running ahead.

Rural life is reflected in calling a switch a "gate," the use of a switch being much like the use of a gate. Back down on the farm, the gate is opened, the wagon and team, tractor, truck, or stock is driven through the gate, and then the gate is closed. Just so on the railroad. The switch is opened, the train moves through, and the switch is relined. To move from the main track through the switch into the siding is to "head in." The siding is the "pass" or the "passing track."

When the train moves out onto the main track (main line) and the hogger gets it up to a fast rate of speed, the train is then "wound up and in the wind."

Procedures for handling air brakes come in for their portion of picturesque names. To slow down, a hoghead "puts the wind under them." To stop in an emergency, he "big holes them," or "puts them in the big hole," or "wipes the clock," the latter term stemming from the resemblance of the air gauge in the engine cab to a brass clock and the rapid movement of the hand from about ninety pounds to zero.

Before the advent of radios, the official signals for communicating between crew members were defined and illustrated in the Book of Rules. The engineer communicated by blowing whistle signals. Other crew members used hand signals. When the engineer was ready to move the train, he gave two short blasts on the whistle ("whistled off"). If everything was ready on the hind end, the answer was a "highball" which was performed by raising a lantern an arm's length above the head, then describing a forward arc with it down to the knee level. When a trainman was anxious to hurry along, the lantern was extended an arm's length above the head, swung in two or three tight horizontal circles, and then arced swiftly downward. This might be repeated a couple of times to say, "Go! Let's get moving!" Another form of highball is used when the head end can't see signals from the cab because of a curve or trees or fog. In such case, the hind man lights a fusee and throws it high into the air. The opposite of the "hurry up" kind of highball is the "washout," or emergency stop signal. With the lantern held at arm's length overhead, the trainman described an arc, not forward, but sideward to knee level. This was repeated as often as was necessary to catch the attention of the head end. An engineer approaching a station would "blow" a meet, two short and one prolonged blast of the whistle. To indicate using the main track, a single long blast, not prolonged, was used.

The many hand signals and their appropriateness would make a Kiowa chief smile. While some were prescribed by management, most came into being through the insight of employees. One was the "whiskers" sign. When a company officer is about, a simple, quick, beard-stroking motion alerts others to his presence. If the officer happens to have big feet, he is positively identified with the beard stroke and any motion of the foot which will attract a quick glance.

When a train is made up in a yard, assuming a ninety-pound air pressure train line, the car knocker watches the air gauge on the caboose, and when seventy-five pounds of brake pressure is reached (no more than a fifteen-pound loss between engine and cab is permissible), he stands by the caboose facing the engine, extends an arm upward full length, and motions crosswise to the track several times. The engineer then sets the air. When set, the car knocker holds his hand up full length. The air is then released, after which the car knocker gives a highball-like signal called the "high sign."

Other hand signals include the following:

Couple up—Hold elbows out with hands formed in half fists to represent two couplers; then bring hands together as though the "couplers" are moving into one another.

12. HAND, FLAG AND LAMP SIGNALS

MANNER OF USING	INDICATION	
(a) Swung at right angles to track.	Stop.	
(b) Slight horizontal movement at arm's length at right angles to track.	Reduce speed.	
(c) Raised and lowered vertically.	Proceed. Trainmen's Answer to 14 (k).	
(d) Swung vertically in a circle at right angles to track.	Back.	

From the author's copy of Rules and Regulations of the Transportation Department, Southern Pacific Lines, Effective February 15, 1943.

14.   ENGINE WHISTLE SIGNALS

Note—The signals prescribed are illustrated by "o" for short sounds; "—" for longer sounds. The sound of the whistle should be distinct, with intensity and duration proportionate to the distance signal is to be conveyed.

Steam whistle will be used in sounding signals, except that when engine is so equipped, air whistle instead of steam whistle will be used in sounding signals 14 (*l*) and 14 (*p*).

SOUND	INDICATION
(*a*) o	Apply brakes. Stop.
(*b*) — —	Release brakes. Proceed. Must be given after stopping at a railroad crossing not protected by an interlocking.
(*c*) — o o o	Flagman protect rear of train.
(*c-a*) o o o —	Flagman protect front of train.
(*d*) — — — —	Flagman may return from west as prescribed by Rule 99.
(*e*) — — — — —	Flagman may return from east as prescribed by Rule 99.
(*f*) — — —	Train parted.
(*g*) o o	Answer to 14 (*k*) or any signal not otherwise provided for. Not to be given in answer to a yellow signal or the explosion of two torpedoes.
(*h*) o o o	When standing, back. Answer to 12 (*d*) and 16 (*c*). When running, answer to 16 (*d*).
(*j*) o o o o	Call for signals.

Making a joint (coupling air hoses)—Hold both arms out from sides and at a somewhat downward angle; then allow them to swing together at the bottom of the circle, making a picture of dangling air hoses being brought together.

Forward movement—When the highball previously described is done slowly, this signal indicates "ease ahead," or "slowly," with more speed indicated by more vigorous execution of the signal.

Backward movement—The hand signal is performed by moving the hand in a circle. Back easy is a small circle with hand moving slowly. The faster the motion desired, the wider the circle and the faster the movement.

Kicking a car into another track involves getting up speed quickly, detaching the car, and letting the momentum keep it rolling while the engine brakes. To stop or slow the move, the hand or lantern is swung out to the side, stopped at a point about waist high, followed by a brief pause, then downward toward the knee and back, making such movement two or three times.

Head in—Touch head, point at an angle toward the track to be entered.

Back in—Tap back of left hand with palm of right hand.

Take water—This signal is given with the hand up, palm forward, fingers curled to palm, thumb to mouth in drinking gesture. It is a hitch-hiker sign, except the thumb is to mouth.

Time to eat—Both hands are raised, fingers curved, both thumbs to mouth to represent a fellow so starved that he is eating with both hands.

Pick up (add cars)—Forearms are held horizontal to the ground and extending forward, hands with palms down formed in loose fists, as if picking up some object. Also, palms can be up and close to chest and upward motion made.

Track signals. House track (the house track runs next to the depot)—The signal is made with the hands over the head, extended fingers touching, making a house top. Cotton mill track—Make a circular motion as though grinding coffee in a coffee mill. Stock pen track—Place hands alongside head with palms forward, fingers extended upward. Spur track—Grasp the foot on its heel.

Movement of switches and derails. Line the switch—Point left index finger to ground and make several circles, all the while pointing with right hand to the particular switch to be lined. Lock it up (lock the switch)—With elbows out, pump right fist into left palm. Line the derail—This signal is made with the forearm horizontal to the ground and forward, hand open, fingers straight with thumb lying along forefinger (the hand looks prepared for a karate chop). From the wrist, rotate the hand back and forth in flip-flop motion.

Condition of cars. Hot box (overheated wheel bearings)—Hold nose between thumb and forefinger. Hand brake set, needs to be released—Make a motion as though moving the steering wheel of an automobile (freight cars are equipped with "steering" wheels located on one end of the car body which turn to set or release hand brakes). Brakes sticking, sliding wheels—With the elbows near body, forearms horizontal and forward, palms down, and fingers extended, make sliding motion forward.

"Slack action" and "slack" are a very vital part of train movement. Each car is built so that it has five inches of free slack and five of spring slack, that is, ten inches of play between cars. An engineer takes the slack, starting the cars one by one and tightening the slack between cars. This is the secret to starting heavy trains: the cars are started one by one. If the train stops on a grade with the slack stretched, it becomes necessary to back up and bunch the slack so that the head end can stretch them again. When diesel units made possible such long trains, the slack action running in and out frequently injured the men riding the caboose. Just think, a train of one hundred cars moving ten miles an hour suddenly stops. The caboose is still moving, and will do so for ten inches per car for one hundred cars (990 inches), then stop like striking a brick wall. Many ribs were taped by doctors, and many were the bruises suffered before the company finally provided specially designed cabooses to cope with this.

Early steam engines were built with long levers called Johnson bars right in front of the engineer's seat. The lever connected to the reversing mechanism which also determined the degree of tractive power applied. It was necessary to stand to move it. An engineman wanting to move forward pulling moderate tonnage would move the lever along its forward arc to a point about midway the arc. If more tonnage were to be moved or a grade to be pulled, he would place it farther down. He got more pull this way, and less speed. Raising the lever as the train pulled more easily gave more speed. Then he was "hooking them up." The lever was the "strong arm," and after technology replaced the Johnson bar with a small lever which pivoted along a notch quadrant placed handily at the hoghead's side, the name "strong arm" transferred to the new device. When the hogger was gathering running speed quickly, or trying to maintain speed on a grade, he would notch the lever down a bit and widen out on the throttle. Then the exhaust became sharper and louder, and it was said that "he's knocking the stack off her." Pulling a grade on slick rail could cause the drivers to spin and the engine to "fall" down unless the rails were sanded. The engineer released sand which flowed through tubes from the sand box down around the drivers to just a couple of inches above the rail. The sand would flow right on the rail ahead of the surface of the driver so long as the wind was not too strong. In order to maintain comfort for passengers, passenger engineers would keep the cars stretched by braking against power, that is, breaking against steam. Such a stop is a "passenger train stop." Freight engineers weren't usually so careful.

An engineer was "cannonballing," or "stonewalling," when he was working his engine unnecessarily hard, knocking the stack off to no purpose. This wastes fuel and water and makes an engineer unpopular with the fireman because his workload is increased. Firemen lacking the know-how of keeping a clean fire caused soot to form in the flues, making sanding the flues necessary. This was done by the engineer cannonballing for a short distance, thus creating a strong draft through the firebox while the fireboy shoveled sand into the firebox. The grains of sand swirled along the flues, cutting the sticky soot which clung to the grains of sand as they exited the stack and showered to the ground. One should never stand near the track in good clothing when the crew is sanding the flues.

"Mud" (coffee) was poured into syrup bottles at home and brought to work and placed on the boiler head of the engine. Syrup bottles were made of a thicker glass than were most containers. The mud was set on the boiler head and heated for drinking. The invention of thermos bottles did away with this practice, but the memory lingered on for some. One day when his train was in the siding for an opposing movement, a fireman ran across the track and adjacent street to a grocery and bought two cans of chili and beans, then ran back to his engine and placed them on the boiler head to heat. About that time the train met its opposition and pulled out. The fireman busied himself with his job and forgot about the cans whose tops he had failed to puncture. When the cans exploded, it was like the sound of a double-barreled shotgun when both triggers are squeezed, and chili and beans flew all over the deck.

There are two practices which are forbidden by the rules. They are seldom done because they are such high risks. One is the "Dutch drop." A drop is made when it is necessary to place a car which is behind the engine in a one-ended track whose switch opens toward the engine. This is accomplished by speeding up the engine, detaching the car, and letting it roll while the engine races past the switch. The switch is thrown, and the rolling car rolls into the track. This movement is within the rules. Now suppose that the car is to be picked up, and rather than head in on the car, drag it out on the main, and shove it ahead of the engine to a double-ended track where it can be run around, the crew elects to make a

Dutch drop. The engine heads in, couples into the car, then races backward. The car is detached and continues under its own momentum. The engine must get on the main, the switch must be lined so that the engine can race down the main track past the switch and the rolling car, and the switch relined in time for the rolling car to move through the switch and onto the main track behind the engine.

"Smoking," or "smoking a meet," is the other unsafe action. Before telephones, there would be instances where one train would hold orders to meet another train at, say, station D, and would sit there for hours wondering what had happened to the other train which was also being delayed. The crew, unable to telephone or radio the dispatcher and get authority to move, might find a track person with a track car to carry their flagman ahead of them to the next siding, or if the distance to station C was not too far for walking, send the head man walking ahead with flagging equipment to station C. But sometimes they would smoke to C, that is, the fireman would get all the smoke he could going from the stack, and with this big smoke signal, the train would move to station C, hoping that if the opposing train should appear, he would see the signal and lay back. In such an instance, the crew of the other train, rather than turn in the smoking crew and get them fired, might conveniently have air-brake trouble and not reach station C until the smoking crew had their train in the clear. By the 1930s and 1940s, highways often paralleled track, and a flagman would hail a motorist and ride to station C to flag his opposition. This was still called smoking. Radios have all but eliminated the conditions which would give rise to such a move.

A "cornfield" meet can happen when a crew overlooks or misreads a train movement instruction (train order) or runs a red block. One night, First 249 received this order: "First 249 has right over Second 248 Hearne Jct. to Dime Box and wait at Mumford until 12:15 A.M. for Second 248." Before clearing the train with orders, the dispatcher conferred with the yardboss and found First 249 might not be on it, and so he issued this order: "First 249 wait at Mumford until 12:35 A.M. for Second 248." There were no block signals on the Dalsa between Giddings and Hearne. First 249 left Hearne about 12:15 A.M., and the entire crew forgot the 12:35 A.M. wait at Mumford, but the crew on Second 248 did not. No one was seriously injured in that one, but it took several days to clear the wreck.

The Federal Hours of Service Act provides that train-order operators and towermen work no more than nine hours before taking rest and that train crews work no more than twelve hours. The time used to be sixteen hours and was referred to in the press as the sixteen-hour law. When a crew can't make the next terminal within its twelve hours, the crew "ties up on the law," or "ties up on the hogs," or "the hogs get them," and they go off duty and deadhead to their tie-up point.

Most crews work on a "chain gang" or "pool turn" basis. That is, there will be, let us say, twelve crews assigned to the Dalsa, each crew being called in its turn for service. This gives rise to "run arounds," when one crew passes another for some reason, and the members of the crew which is run around feel they have been bilked because the amount of money that they stand to make in the year is diminished each time that they are run around. The company has made agreements with the unions which pretty well offset the economic effects of run arounds, but crews still feel mistreated when run around. There are work assignments to which pool crews are subject which the men dislike and which a number try to dodge. This dodging is called "sharp practice," and when a person resorts to laying off work in order to dodge the job, he is reported not as having "layed by" (laid off), but as having "lied by."

The men who patrol the track each day are known as "road runners." The term "King Snipe" (foreman) doesn't get much usage, though "gandy dancer" (track laborer) is pretty common. The first thing to do at a derailment is to "shoo-fly" around it, that is, build a temporary track so that traffic can continue while the derailment is being cleared. When a rail is found broken near one end, the broken end may be cut off, new bolt holes drilled, and a short piece of rail called a "Dutchman" installed. Doing this saves money, but the FRA (Federal Railroad Administration) now prohibits the practice on main tracks.

Living and working in a railroad environment is somewhat like living and working in the military, and just as there are "latrine rumors" in the army and "scuttlebutt" in the navy, there is "sandhouse" on the railroad.

"Standing up and black" is a term of good news. During daylight hours, crews keep watch for the safety of the train as it runs between terminals, the head end watching back along the line of cars, the hind end watching ahead. Track maintenance crews also "look 'em over" while the train is passing and if nothing amiss is seen, the train is waved on. What about night operations? Though the crews watch, they can't see very well and depend on seeing sparks from steel striking steel if a car derails or if equipment is dragging or depend on seeing a glow of hot metal or a flame if a journal is running hot. By the time sparks fly or metal flames, it may be too late to do anything other than to take emergency action. Therefore, spark or flame spells bad news for the crew running at night, but their absence, i.e., all "standing up and black," is the assurance that all is well and the train is in no danger.

Railroaders enjoy their lingo. It has been created by the many unlearned verbal artists whose names have been carried on countless payrolls in the past, and it will continue being created by those modern-day verbal artists whose names are on today's payrolls. By using this language freely in their everyday communications, employees identify with their calling and with each other. In one extreme case, one hoghead (not on the S.P.) identified so strongly with his calling that he applied railroad jargon to the many non-railroad things and occurrences in his life. His legs were "drivers" and his stomach was the "boiler," etc. His is the extreme case. But, if you should converse with an Espee employee about the recent rail tragedy in Maryland where a Conrail freight engine and an

Southern Pacific passenger train 16; photo taken in Dallas by Ford Curry. *From the William J. Neill Collection.*

Amtrak passenger train collided, injuring many and killing others, including the Amtrak engineer who jumped to his death, that employee will tell you that until the reports from the investigations are in, we won't know just what took place. But he will tell you: "This much we understand: The Conrail job had made town, the crew had put the train away, and the head shack was bringing the enjine around to the tie-up track. The Conrail hoghead was backing three units, and the head man was riding the rear unit and communicating with his walkie talkie. Something went wrong; they ran a red block, and the rear unit moved out on the main just a second or two ahead of the varnished cars. There was no time for the Amtrak hoghead to big hole 'em; he left that for the dead man feature, and he joined the birds."

KENNETH W. DAVIS

Mechanical Macho
The Current Craze for Customizing Pickups

Partisan owners of Chevrolet, GMC, or Dodge pickups may disagree with television commercials which proclaim Texas "Ford Country," but most pickup owners believe that for convenience and dependability these vehicles are the best on the road. No parking lot in the Southwest is without its share of pickups in many colors, shapes, sizes, and degrees of customization. Owners of these utilitarian as well as recreational vehicles are high school students, attorneys, farmers, plumbers, ranchers, and schoolteachers. In Lubbock, some wealthy physicians supplement their stables of Mercedes SLs with elaborately customized pickups.

Like people who drive ordinary cars, pickup owners lavish money and attention on their prized vehicles to customize them. Most owners insist that they add expensive extras to pickups for purely practical reasons. Many other pickup drivers will admit, however, that they customize their vehicles for a variety of aesthetic reasons. Some of the reasons given for customizing suggest the presence of an emerging—or, more likely, a surviving—macho syndrome reminiscent of attitudes found in early western fiction as well as in works by Zane Grey and Louis L'Amour.

I will consider macho aspects, but first I must note some of the supposed reasons for replacing plastic grills with ones made of stainless steel. Then, I will suggest the real reasons for spending from one hundred to three or four thousand dollars on other modifications to make a pickup something it wasn't when it left Detroit or wherever the subtle art of human workers and robots made a thing that can become an extension of its owner's personality.

I gathered information from a number of redoubtable experts. Youths in auto parts stores supplied many details. These people read with phenomenal accuracy mysterious numbers in parts catalogs. Such worthies in the transportation chain may not appreciate the pathos in "Bonny Barbara Allen," but they will almost always sell a customer the right Allen wrench. A second group of informants included employees in shops which specialize in customizing vans and pickups. These informants, too, were sources of all but unbelievable amounts of information about this form of artistry. And, of course, I talked with owners of customized pickups. I visited with them at truck stops, in parking lots, and on the premises of pickup dealerships in Texas and in New Mexico.

After spending one hundred dollars or more to install a new stainless steel grill to replace the factory's more expensive plastic one, and after adding running boards complete with courtesy lights, a ventilated tailgate, and a sliding rear window, a customizer can say with a perfectly straight face that he did all of this work for practical reasons. The steel grill won't break as easily as the plastic one if the pickup meets an obstruction such as a slow-moving cow, deer, goat, or a stationary mesquite tree. A running board is essential for hired hands or rabbit shooting buddies to stand on. A ventilated tailgate reduces wind resistance and therefore increases gas mileage significantly—or so I was solemnly assured by a rancher from Post, Texas. At one shop, I saw the "literature" from the maker of these fancy tailgates. This advertising sheet suggested, but did not actually claim, better mileage from pickups equipped with these sometimes splendidly chromed devices. I didn't ask my informants how a tailgate with movable slats in it would serve at a tailgate party before a football game. You may remember the irreverent account of such a party in Dan Jenkins's *Baja Oklahoma.* Tailgate parties are all

Oversized tires, the double toolchest, blinds, and the custom-designed rear bumper mark this truck as a heavily customized one. Note the ventilated tail gate, which is supposed to raise gasoline mileage and may also serve the utilitarian purpose of allowing fluids that the bed captures to escape before causing rust or corrosion damage.

This imported pickup looks like a standard model, but the chromed wheels for the oversized tires, the black non-reflective side mirrors, and the camper shell are all specially added items.

the rage now. In Lubbock, home of a state university, a special section of the stadium parking lot is set aside for pickup owners who convene, prior to the afternoon's carnage on the football field, for close fellowship whilst eating barbeque, potato salad, many kinds of gelatinous substances, and fried pies. But, as Byron said, "I digress."

The utilitarian functions of sliding back-windows are complex and prompted some of the most interesting of the attempts at justification. One rancher said he used the sliding window to keep the pickup cab cool. Another man explained that having a sliding window gave him a gun port for shooting coyotes and other varmints. I found the image of a portly adult twisting around to shoot from a rear window a bit puzzling, but I thought a discussion with a fellow who had two rifles in his pickup's chromed gun racks would be impolite, or imprudent, or, at best, inopportune.

All arguments that practical considerations motivate people to customize pickups are sincere, but a prosperous farmer from north of Lubbock may have said more than he knew he was saying when he came into a customizer's shop to get his Sierra, which had been moderately customized with a classically simple stainless steel grill, discreet running boards with subdued courtesy lights, and a ventilated tailgate painted to match exactly the color of the pickup. He took a long look at what the shop's modern Cellinis had done with wrenches and paint-guns. Then, to no one in particular, he said: "Damn! That's slick. The wife's goin' to like that a bunch."

This expression of joy contains a key to a great deal of interesting lore. Advertising chiefs in New York long ago began to use psychological factors to sell everything. A vast body of such lore pertains to selling pickups. Some of that lore conveys the notion that a pickup is a reflection of the image the buyer has of himself—or the image of himself (or herself) the buyer wishes to project. The well-to-do farmer who so admired the cosmetic changes in his recently purchased plain vanilla Sierra probably felt a nice surge of machismo as he gazed at the gleaming truck with its freshly done face-lift and other body work.

Farmers and ranchers—the settled as well as the restless types—share with city folks some of the same reasons for buying and customizing pickups. The city folks I refer to include teenagers as well as those sometimes described by that obnoxious word from the recent political campaign: "yuppies." Young professionals customize pickups for some of the reasons pickup-worshipping teenagers spend all they earn to make works of art of ordinary Ford, Chevrolet, Dodge, or GMC pickups. Lest I be accused of jingoism, I will note parenthetically that in Hobbs, New Mexico, there is a club whose membership is limited to owners of customized Toyota pickups. In Lubbock, however, I found few foreign-made pickups that had been customized. I asked one body man about the scarcity of customized imported pickups. His response, "Oh, them thangs." I didn't ask a follow-up question.

One customizing touch which appeals to farmers, teenagers, and yuppies requires the application of thin sheets of a dark plastic substance to the windows of pickups—side and back—to darken the interiors. An auto parts store manager told me that this practice is totally practical. The dark gray or brown sheets reduce the sun's fading of upholstery; they also keep out the relentless heat rays and thus help prevent overheating of the interior. But the real reason for the darkening of windows came from a high school student who carries my groceries out to my car each week. His respect for me grew immensely when in late December of 1983 I bought a new Bronco II. When I asked him why he so admired the factory-installed dark glass on the sides and at the rear of my Bronco, he responded, "Man, that's cool." He wasn't referring to temperature; instead, he was expressing the sort of admiration people have had for their modes of transportation since long before the days when Roman charioteers pampered their horses.

What can be done to customize a pickup by a modern

knight or urban cowboy? Here is an abbreviated list of some of the major bits of decoration or plumage available to make a pickup, and by association, its owner, attractive, knightly, courtly, or heroic.

1. The previously mentioned stainless steel grills and the chromed or merely painted ventilated tailgates;

2. running boards, some illuminated with courtesy lights;

3. bed mats (rubber mats to prevent heavy objects from scarring either the floor or the sides of the pickup's cargo section);

4. plexiglass bug deflectors in a variety of attractive colors as well as the clear ones;

5. bucket seats, some boasting orthopaedic design;

6. sun roofs, for star gazing, for use on hunting expeditions, or for pleasant moonlit drives; and,

7. loud pipes. Many folks past fifty would call "loud pipes" by an older name, "Schmitties," or even "glass packs." These satanic inventions can broadcast throughout residential sections harmonally urged yawps which humans make with engine exhaust. Birds know better; they sing. In my sedate and somewhat fading middle-class neighborhood, most of the residents of a two-block area considered the collective purchase of a gift when one of the area's more nubile maidens finally married and thus caused an end to the nightly processions of young swains with roaring exhausts who drove frantically around the blocks in a courting ritual which resembled the mating dance of prairie chickens shown in a Walt Disney nature film a decade or two ago. We didn't really buy a present, but we all earnestly hope that the marriage will last forever in Alaska, the state to which the newlyweds migrated.

But, back to the nuts and bolts. What are some of the relatively inexpensive items available for under fifty dollars to embellish a pickup? Chromed exhaust extenders, plastic sunshield murals for rear windows, mud flaps, steering wheel covers, and floor mats of varied colors are available in this price range. All of these items are more cosmetic than essential, but as Lear said, "Reason not the need."

This customized truck features a chromed-rod grill. These grills—perhaps the most popular item used in customizing—are good-looking and provide greater protection to the vehicle's radiator. Note the difference between the chromed-rod grill and the standard grill on the right.

Outstanding features of this customized pickup include the paint job, the chrome strips along the sides, and the carefully scrubbed tires.

That teenagers, yuppies of various ages, and rural types customize pickups to enhance personal image is obvious to me. Other aspects of pickup lore are equally interesting.

In one parts store, I chatted with an initially diffident young man who told me that although owners of customized pickups don't have a club that he knows of, they do "hang out" together. Such hanging out is a form of male bonding which can lead to the formation of gangs, but my informant insisted that among his loose confederation of fellow pickup owners, some rules are obeyed. No one suspected of using stolen parts or materials is accepted; no one who drinks "too much" is accepted; any person who won't stop to help stranded motorists is unwelcome. He explained the "Good Samaritan" aspect of the code by saying that if pickup drivers who cruise the streets on Friday and Saturday nights didn't work to create good images, they would have problems with the police.

I then asked him if he knew of girls who customized pickups. He had heard of a couple of girls who "were into customizing," but added that he hadn't met them. I asked if he and his group would welcome the presence of girls. "Not exactly," was his response; then he added, "We like to get away from the girls now and then and just talk pickups." Thus it ever was. "Buddies in the Saddle"—the title of a song by A. P. Carter—suggested bonds of interest that linked cowboys. The line indirectly glosses an aspect of pickup lore also.

Another high school student told me of a friend of his who customized his pickup as a project in his industrial education course. This student entered and won first prize in an area-wide contest. This fact points to social approval or acceptance of activities which exist broadly in a sort of subculture.

When I interviewed the younger informants, particularly the high school students, I made casual references to lore Jan Harold Brunvand has treated so well in his book *The Vanishing Hitchhiker.* I asked about stories of phantom pickups, those double cousins, perhaps, to the Phantom 409 that Red Sovine memorialized. Among pickup customizers today, there isn't much interest in lore with such honorable ancestry as mysterious horsemen who "evanished" at dawn. One young man, a literate sort, had heard of stories about ghostly semi-trucks. He thought that he also remembered something about a driverless pickup that appears only on foggy nights in April, but he quickly assured me that all such stories are "just a pack of foolishness from TV or somewhere." Even so, I intend to keep checking now and then. I'd like to know more about a phantom customized GMC that manifests itself on foggy nights at any time of the year.

Other facets of lore about customizing pickups deserve mention. We all know how young males want to make their cars distinctive, unique. Tom Wolfe has written about this phenomenon in California. In the world of pickup customizing, there is an almost exactly opposite intent. With a sleek new stainless steel grill, the front end of a GMC is the same as the front end of a Chevrolet or a Ford—or, in some instances, it is the same as the front end of a Dodge. Customizers of Dodge pickups usually leave the distinctive chromed ram as a hood ornament for reasons I will leave to the social and cultural anthropologists.

I do not suggest that herd thinking or impulses toward mass conformity are behind all the similarities, but I am curious about the matter. Could it be that the desire for anonymity or privacy which makes darkened windows essential also makes pickup customizers long to efface their identities behind grills that look alike? I had begun to think that I was reaping some esoteric benefit from premature senility when I first noticed the similarities among the front ends of pickups. I asked a brusque but friendly lady of indeterminate age—owner of a parts store—why so many customized pickups are identical. She set me straight and eased my mind. She stubbed out a lethal, pencil-thin cigar and said: "Hell, son, don't worry none. It's just the way them grills come from the factory." She added, "But if it bugs you, ask some of them smart bastards at the university; they think they know it all." (In my interviews, I was careful not to identify myself as a college professor.)

Scriptures tell us that we must become as little children if we are to enter the kingdom of Heaven. The great poets of the Romantic era venerated the uncorrupted wisdom of children. To begin a conclusion to my remarks, I turn to the world of children for a significant bit of lore. We all remember the magic formulaic opening that transported us to wondrous lands and let us have imaginary friends long before Puff the Magic Dragon came along. We simply said "Play like . . ." and we were off like the poet with his eye in a fine frenzy rolling. We played cowboys and Indians, cops and robbers, and whatever else we fancied.

In Lubbock, the many "windshield" farmers have inspired a new "play-like" fantasy game for children. A windshield farmer is one who lives within the city limits among gaggles of schoolteachers, plumbers, attorneys, and so on. Farmers who live on the land sometimes make slighting references to their city-dwelling peers and accuse them of spending more time driving around looking through windshields than actually farming. But to active young sons of pale-faced, bespectacled, and briefcase-laden lawyers, accountants, college professors, and even physicians, these deeply tanned windshield farmers are present-day knights, explorers, adventurers, and cowboys in command of shining symbols of utter power. These modern-day paladins roar out in the early mornings to the soul-satisfying sounds of finely tuned loud pipes to spend days outdoors doing marvelous and mysterious things such as feeding cattle, driving tractors, or riding horses. The exploits of these Herculean folks become for small boys the stuff of fantasy or play-like games of Homeric proportions. A colleague of mine, father of two boys, was curious about the fact that his sons and their buddies staged lengthy, serial, play-like games devoted to mythical adventures of pickup owners. I see nothing curious in this phenomenon; I can recall play-like games that occupied every recess and noon hour in grade school. We kept such epic stories alive for weeks.

The fact that children sense machismo, or heroic behavior—call it what you will—in drivers of customized pickups

This pickup features sturdy chrome roll bars, expensive halogen "fog" lights, and added chrome as well as the mandatory custom paint job. Notice also the sliding rear window panel.

Note the carefully upholstered seats, the thick carpets, and the steering wheel cover in this pickup's interior. The steering wheel cover matches the upholstery of the seats and serves to protect the wheel from the penetrating heat of the West Texas sun.

supports my thesis that behind all the supposed practical reasons for customizing pickups, there survives an abiding tradition, perhaps a healthy biological impulse, which prompts the male of the species to strut a bit, to show his plumage to impress other males, and eventually, to try to be deemed worthy of the more intelligent sex, the females. But never mind so much theorizing; the fact remains: a well-customized pickup really does look good. Some hyacinths for the soul appear as chromed bumpers, stainless grills, roll bars, and ventilated tailgates.

As a brief coda, I can report that on the afternoon when I finished interviewing the fifty or so informants who gave me information for this paper, I saw what is surely the ultimate pickup. But because it was a conversion and not a customization job, I excluded mention of it until now. This supremely beautiful pickup was fashioned from a Lincoln Continental. What a lot of loving surgery with a cutting torch was required to make a once-proud, four-door sedan into the most elegant of pickups. The customizing was done with such consummate skill that the vehicle looked factory designed and factory fresh. This pickup reflected a perfect, if not fearful symmetry. I hoped the owners would look like Bo Derek and Robert Redford. Alas, they were a pleasantly frumpy retired couple out buying groceries on double-stamp day like the rest of us.

At some time in the future there should be a report on the special language customizers of pickups use. At present, a discrete lingo for this craft is developing slowly. The interviewer who collects such examples of folk speech will have to spend many hours in auto parts stores and in customizing shops. And, of course, the interviewer will need a good straw hat and maybe some sunshades. Much of the skillful artistry I have mentioned today is done shade-tree fashion.

All photographs reproduced by permission of Kenneth Davis.

JACK WELCH

Texas Baptistry Paintings
Landscape, Doctrine, Mysticism

Although unstudied and unheralded, a type of distinctly American landscape painting has developed in some Baptist churches, Churches of Christ, Christian Churches, and Disciples of Christ churches. These churches, to which a sizeable majority of Texans belong, usually have no other art in their meeting places and are known primarily for their down-to-earth dependence upon words for religious instruction. All the paintings have been placed in the front of the church auditorium behind the pulpit and above the baptistries. The paintings are all landscapes. None of the Texas paintings in this study contain any people or structures; rarely is there conventional religious symbolism. The paintings are scattered uniformly throughout the cities, towns, villages, and crossroads of Texas as well as in other parts of the United States.

All the paintings have water which gives the illusion of flowing into the baptistry from a creek, river, or lake. Around the water are land and flora which enrich the artistic experience for the congregation which, in full view of the painting, will be singing, praying, and listening to sermons. Although American churches have not directly imitated ancient Christian church buildings in this regard, it is interesting to observe that the oldest known Christian church building was located in Dura-Europos in Syria. This was a house church because in 230 A.D., when it is believed that the building was converted into Christian use, Christianity was illegal in the Roman empire. In one room of this building archeologists unearthed an ancient baptistry which had watermarks on it indicating that about a meter of water was kept in the pool for baptisms. Above this pool was a baptistry painting with water in the painting beginning at the water of the pool and flowing back into a body of water in the painting. Sheep are in and around the pool; reeds or rushes can still be discerned in the area of the painting's water. Above it all is a man with a sheep on his shoulders; he has short hair and is wearing a common Roman tunic. He is the Good Shepherd, familiar in the Gospels and in early Christian art. Although this primitive painting is not a direct ancestor of the American baptistry paintings, it provides a powerful precedent, suggesting that religious and sociological factors which influenced the third century are still at work in the Texas churches.

The artists who created these paintings range in training from the primitive to the university educated. They were frequently members of the congregations in whose buildings the paintings were hung. A majority of them were women, and it is impossible to distinguish their works from those of the men who painted the same subjects.

The Texas baptistry paintings may be divided into three broad categories of ascending abstraction. The most obvious of the categories is literal realism; the paintings provide artistic insights into how Texas is viewed by its local artists. Next, the paintings suggest something about the moral doctrine connected with baptism. Finally, and most surprisingly, the paintings reveal a symbolical mysticism which could be compared to the anagogical level of Christian literary criticism which was developed in the Middle Ages.

On the most literal level, the Texas baptistry paintings are valuable because they provide a state-wide cycle of twentieth-century landscapes which have no counterpart anywhere else in the state. For example, the painting in the Church of Christ of Clyde, Callahan County, strikes one first of all with its western quality. The water in the foreground comes from a wide, shallow river which meanders from the background where a formidable mesa towers over the river

Church of Christ, Clyde, Texas.

valley. Cottonwood trees along the river and desert shrubs along the sides of the mesa comprise the major flora of the painting. The sky at the top of the painting is light blue, but clouds hang gray and somber in the middle sky. One of the members of the congregation, Mr. Buford Hailey, a former county agent in the area, suggested that the yellow sky just below the clouds was created by a West Texas dust storm. Mr. Hailey may well be correct, but in other baptistry paintings in the east the yellow sky has been air pollution. The question then arises whether the yellow is a realistic depiction of the environment, a pigmental choice to allow a certain brightness in the painting, or both. The Clyde painting was done by Bill Seffmich in 1977. The western quality which this painting emphasizes is the vast openness of the country. The absence of people and animals (in keeping with the American tradition of the baptistry painting) intensifies the power of the countryside as well as heightens the loneliness. The paint for this painting was applied directly to the plaster above the baptistry which is kept filled at all times. This painting is in nearly perfect condition as are almost all the other paintings.

About ten miles south of Sweetwater is another regional landscape, this one done by Sandra Light for the Church of Christ in Maryneal. This painting has water from a modest-sized river which reflects the cumulus cloud cover of the sky. Only a few cedar-like trees line this river, some of which actually grow in the hilly territory south of Sweetwater. The distant hills in the painting lack any flora. The first impression given by this painting is of infertility and emptiness, but the heavy cloud cover, which is intensified by its reflection in the water, promises the blessing of rainfall which in this part of Texas is continually hoped and prayed for. Thus the painting suggests the promise of growth just as the immersion in the baptismal water promises spiritual growth to the parched soul. The painting was done in 1958 shortly after Mrs. Light moved to Maryneal. Although the building in which the congregation previously had worshipped had no baptistry painting, the congregation asked Mrs. Light to paint this one. She indicated in an interview that this painting was her own conception of the Jordan River. The painting is about seven feet by six feet and is oil paint on masonite.

In San Antonio at the Baptist Temple is a third painting which reflects the Texas landscape, this time the beautiful Texas hill country. Mrs. Helen Ferne Slimp painted the work in 1947 when she and her husband were still active members of the congregation. Born in 1890, Mrs. Slimp in an interview concerning her painting said that her goal in painting the work was to do some kind of likeness of Jordan. She looked at snapshots of the river given to her by friends, but she never could use them. "So," she said, "I designed my own River Jordan. It looked just like Texas." Mrs. Slimp is a native Virginian, but she has lived her adult life in Texas. Some of her other landscapes were chosen for calendar paintings, and as a result of her frequent use of the bluebonnets in her landscapes, she became known as "the bluebonnet painter." Mrs. Slimp studied art with Gerald Cassidy in Santa Fe and with Boardman Robinson in Colorado Springs. In addition to having done several baptistry paintings, she designed stained-glass windows for several congregations in Texas.

The Baptist Temple painting depicts the vast Texas sky with a few clouds enriching the horizon. The river which flows into the baptistry comes with canal-like directness from the horizon. Beside the river, a live oak tree has been painted in its full maturity and vigor. Because the rolling hills, the yellow grass, and the live oak all accurately represent the hill country just north of San Antonio, the painting seems to be asserting that the blessings of baptism are available in this time and in this place. The Jordan River provided the means of obtaining salvation for those of that place, but Texas provides its own places of salvation for those of this time and place.

Doctrine involved in baptism is suggested in some of the Texas paintings, but even this is not without precedent. In the Dura-Europos painting there is an insert of Adam and Eve in the lower left section of the painting, indicating man's sin

Baptist Temple, San Antonio, Texas.

and baptism's remedy. In the Texas paintings, the doctrinal statements are integrated into the whole design of the paintings by showing contrasting sides of the rivers in which the candidate is to be baptized. For example, in Burnet, Texas, Mona Williams in 1951 painted a river leading back into some treeless mountains. On the right of the river is an open field with short meadow grass suggested in it. However, on the left is a formidable tree with dark green leaves. The general palette for this painting is pastel blue, in keeping with much of the popular painting and house furnishings of the period. However, the tree is far from pastel. Because this tree has a kind of darkness about it, my interpretation is that the tree of the painting is the tree in Eden whose fruit was forbidden but was irresistible to the first couple. Thus the tree represents sin, and the area beyond the river represents the saved state. The technique of this painting and of all the others that deal with the doctrinal possibilities is not realistic; that is, the painting does not seem to have been done in the open countryside or done with a photograph in front of the artist. This painting's pastel colors and stylized leaves and mountains suggest an internal vision rather than a concrete landscape. This painting is considered somewhat old-fashioned by the minister of the congregation, who has had a wooden screen built over the baptismal pool thus partially obscuring the painting as well as anyone who is baptized.

A somewhat similar two-sided effect can be found in a painting which once hung in a building in which the Church of Christ in Clyde met for many years. Now the painting hangs in the residence of Mr. John Estes of Clyde. Although dark in tone, this painting vibrates with color and doctrinal suggestions. On one side of the painting one can see some sheep safely grazing within sight of some tall poplar trees. On the right of the river is a modest tree, an empty field, and a deep forest. The predominant tone of this painting is dark green and light blue. The sky is the most interesting feature of the painting. It lightens at the horizon, and the ridge of distant blue hills is emphasized, but throughout the blue-gray sky is a persistent pale pink as though the sun is enriching the scene in spite of the generous clouds. Symbolically, the believer, when he is baptized, would be crossing from the empty field to the peaceful flock of the church. Something of the complexity and glory of God could be suggested by the colors of the painting. This painting is rare in that the technique is impressionistic. Nothing is solid mass; everything is shimmering with light. It was done by Jesse Slater.

The most experimental painting in this study is found in the village of Cherokee in Llano County. Here in the Church of Christ building the artist had to confront the problem of a two-part baptistry. The candidate descends a ladder into the back of the baptistry, where the baptism takes place. The artist decided to paint two panels on the front two sides of the baptistry flanking the door. Then she decided to paint a panel above the rear of the baptistry in the area behind the door, creating a Texas baptistry triptych. This painting's composition lends itself to the two-sided, doctrinal interpretation. On the right is a rocky area with leafy trees, as though the area were in a kind of late summer. However, on the left is a wooded area with young trees which look as though they are just coming into bloom. The candidate could be said to be leaving the side which is about to expire, say, on the judgment day, and to be going to the renewed, refreshing area of eternal spring which would be heaven. However, the distant mountains with their treeless sides and the tranquil sea remind one of certain surreal paintings. In addition, the bright yellow of the sky which is reflected strongly in the water adds a note of surreal glory to the painting. Of all the paintings in the study, this one is the most mentally disturbing and the most audacious both in what it attempted to do and in what it was required to do in conquering the unusual arrangement of the baptistry. No one is likely to call this painting beautiful, but it contains a muted, ironical glory. It was signed by Ruby Ray Swope.

The third category of the Texas baptistry paintings is the mystical, the most difficult and the most unexpected category of baptistry paintings. To understand the mystical in art, one may compare it to the term *anagogical*, which in medieval literary studies was used to denote that highest level of interpretation in literature which was reserved for the spiritual. Jerusalem, for example, could be considered as a literal city on the lowest level, as the church on the allegorical or moral level, and as heaven on the spiritual level. In the teachings of the churches where the paintings hang, there is for each saved member a promise of a mystical reunion with God at a day of judgment. These paintings suggest the nature of that reunion and are constructed to allow the person who is being baptized to have a feeling of the coming reunion. For example, in the Church of Christ at Fourth and Elm in Sweetwater, Texas, is a baptistry painting with a three-dimensional effect. The painting covers the area above the rear of the baptistry, the two walls above the sides of the baptistry, and the front of the baptistry walls in the area leading down the stairs on both sides into the baptistry. Furthermore, the Sweetwater painting is done in what would be termed *soft-focus*, if one were using photographic terms. Thus one gets a sense of the ideal of the landscape with particularities totally eliminated. The color scheme is basically a sky blue with plenty of gold added to the meadows of the foreground. The water from the river which is flowing up to the baptistry comes from remote mountains which are caressed with an enticing blue mist. One finds oneself wishing that he or she could follow that water back to its source, where a deep happiness is artistically suggested. In Jewish tradition, as enunciated in Aryeh Kaplan's book *Waters of Eden: The Mystery of the Mikveh,* all waters are said to have originated in Eden. Heaven is Eden's counterpart since it contains that Tree of Life which once flourished in Eden. The apocalyptical words of John aptly describe this painting: "And he showed me a pure river of water of life, clear as crystal, proceeding out of the throne of God and of the Lamb." (Rev. 22:1) The effect of this painting is one of great beauty, and it has been admired and enjoyed by the congregation since it was painted in 1941 by Floy Sue Tansil, now Mrs. Cliff Brothers of Murfreesboro, Tennessee.

In Seymour, Texas, one painter, W. A. Parsons, painted a matching pair of mystical paintings, one at the Calvary Baptist Church and the other the same year at the Church of Christ. The fact that the art of these two congregations is mutually acceptable suggests the underlying religious and sociological similarity as well. Both paintings portray a garden atmosphere with a pleasant path leading off beside the water. The painting at the Calvary Baptist Church is basically a blue and white painting with stylized green bushes and trees arranged in almost formal symmetry. The painting at the Church of Christ is very similar in composition but has a golden quality to it as though a sunrise or sunset has enriched the color tones throughout. A tree with golden, autumnal leaves has also been added to the second painting. The caretaker at

Church of Christ, Seymour, Texas.

the Church of Christ related a story about how one of the elders of the congregation, a man whose wife had died and who had served the congregation for many years, customarily came to the building to sit and contemplate the painting. This behavior suggests an eschatological quality in the paint-ing in which viewers can obtain a reassurance and even an experience of the heavenly state of the faithful.

A title adds to the mystical effect of the remarkable painting at the Church of Christ in Anson, Texas. The artist, Blanche Perry, revealed the title of her painting during an interview at the time of its completion in 1951. She called the painting *The Word of God and the Elect Lady*, an evocative title which invites a spiritual interpretation of the painting. The Lady, Mrs. Perry said, was embodied in the mountains of the painting which, in fact, suggest a woman lying on her back, and the Word can be found in one of the clouds which is a disguised dove, representing the Holy Spirit whose work through the Bible could make it a logical symbol of the Word.

Calvary Baptist Church, Seymour, Texas.

The identification of the Lady is disputed, but in 2 John, chapter 1, a reference is made to an elect lady who could be the church at large or a particular congregation. "The elder unto the elect lady," writes John, "and her children, whom I love in the truth. . . ."

The size of this painting (sixteen and one-half feet tall and about twelve feet broad at the bottom) gives it a Baroque effect, but this painting does not seem to be insisting upon authority as many of the Baroque works did. This painting does insist on a strong experience. The ceiling of the baptistry is painted blue to match the painting. The painting itself extends far back out of the vision of the congregation who would be looking at the painting from their pews. This extension of the painting is probably for the benefit of the candidate who is in the process of being baptized. Incidentally, the painting at Dura-Europos had a blue plaster canopy with stylized stars over the baptistry so that the baptismal experience was similarly controlled.

The Anson painting is predominantly blue in color and depicts tall, steep mountains such as one would find in the Rockies. Up close, one finds bluebirds and flowers nestled among the trees and grass. These birds and flowers cannot be seen by the congregation at its distance, but, again, can be seen by the candidate. The aspen trees in the painting are leaning out over the fresh, rushing waters, forming a natural arch. It is in that arch in the middle of the painting that the slightly disguised dove appears, the most mystical element in the painting. All in all, this painting is a joyous, shimmering celebration; all nature is joined with the members in the congregation to declare praises to God for the salvation that has come to those who are being baptized.

Although the paintings in this essay have been divided into three distinct categories, it is important to note that some baptistry paintings have characteristics of two or even all three of the categories in them. The painting at the Church of Christ in Center, Texas, is mystical, doctrinal, and probably regional as well. The purple mountain in the distance is pointing off toward some ethereal place, the lush tree on the left suggests the rich spirituality of Christianity, and the rockiness of the mountains suggests the far western section of Texas. Contrariwise, there are one or two paintings which have been documented which fit into none of the categories. In Gorman, Texas, for example is a strong, primitive painting whose distant pyramids suggest something cabalistic or Egyptian. Probably this painting was designed merely to provide a pleasant vista, but its strong lines and planes give it a hypnotic, witty power.

The baptistry paintings of Texas testify to the power of art to emerge in societies which have eschewed conventional religious symbols (in this case, crucifixes, saints, angels, etc.) but have developed a new set of religio-artistic symbols which express the emotion and the glory of the Good News in ways that are subtle and original. Not all Texas baptistry paintings have been documented and studied by scholars, but all have been viewed and experienced week after week in congregations and among people who probably have not even thought consciously about the power of the art that is among them. In most cases, only the artists have really known, and they, the unsung artistic heroes and heroines of their congregations, have given to all of us a surprisingly homogeneous cycle of paintings that have made regions, doctrines, and visions visible in ways that only art can approach and that only the humanities can adequately explain. These paintings are works of art which have been approved by their congregational audiences and have artistically extended the vision of all who view them.

All photographs reproduced by permission of Jack Welch.

Love and respect take varied forms on *Día de los Muertos* in the vast democracy of the dead.

JOHN O. WEST

Celebrations of the Dead
Merging Traditions
in the Spanish Southwest

A 1974 newspaper advertise-
ment in El Paso, Texas, reveals evidence of an interesting
merging of traditions in the Spanish Southwest:

> All Souls' Day
> Saturday, November 2
> This year there will be 2 Masses for the dead at Mt. Carmel
> Cemetery: In Spanish (Saturday), the second English
> (Sunday). . . .[1]

This notice, in both English and Spanish, shows a modern
accommodation to the demands of busy people, rather than
strict observance of age-old customs that made clear distinc-
tions between All Saints' Day, November 1, and All Souls'
Day, November 2. This celebration of the mass on Sunday,
November 3, 1974, has no connection historically with All
Souls' Day or the Day of the Dead—*Día de los difuntos* or *Día
de los muertos* in Spanish. In fact, according to *The New
Catholic Encyclopedia,* Sunday *cannot* be celebrated as All
Souls' Day: If November 2 falls on a Sunday, then November
3 becomes All Souls' Day![2] On the other hand, William S.
Walsh reported in 1898 that "the observance of All Souls'
Day . . . was deemed of such importance that in the event of
its falling on Sunday it was ordered not to be postponed till
Monday, as happens with some other festivals, but to take
place on the previous Saturday, so that souls in purgatory

should not have the ministrations in their behalf unnecessarily postponed. Thus All Saints' and All Souls' Days were occasionally celebrated together."[3]

Remembering the dead on special days is a worldwide and long-lived custom. Regardless of culture or religion, people throughout history have paid reverence, in one way or another, to the memories of the spirits of the departed. The American Memorial Day, May 30, is but a faint echo of traditions lingering since prehistoric times. All Souls' Day, says one authority, is a "rehabilitation of a pagan feast." Walsh cites such celebrations "even in China and Japan" carried on under the name Feast of Lanterns.[4]

The Festival of Lanterns (also called Festival for the Spirits of the Dead) continues to be celebrated in Japan as well as among groups of people of Japanese ancestry who have migrated elsewhere. Occurring during the thirteenth through the fifteenth of the seventh lunar month, the date varies considerably by the Gregorian calendar. The 1981 lunar year, for example, began February 5; hence that year the Feast of Lanterns would have taken place early in September.[5] On the thirteenth, favorite foods are placed before family shrines, lanterns are placed in cemeteries, and "welcome fires" are kindled before houses "to light the way homeward for the guests from the other world."[6] The custom, believed to have come from India, also includes a sort of competition in the building of tiny but elaborate boats that are set adrift along rivers with messages for the dead.[7] Then on the final day of the festival, "farewell fires" are lit, which, with the tiny boats, also carrying lights and provisions for the recent dead, form a symbolic link with the other world.[8]

Both concern for the dead and the modern dates—November 1 and 2—were involved in Druid ceremonies called Samhain at year's end. The very word *Samhain* is the word for November and means simply "end of summer."[9] At that time there was a harvest festival and feast. Also involved was a rekindling of altar fires to protect people during the coming winter, and a brief visit home for the souls of the dead was allowed. They came "in search of warmth and comfort as winter approached." [10]

Celebration of the memories of church martyrs apparently began the modern Christian customs surrounding All Saints' and All Souls' days. In the Eastern church, a feast for all martyrs was begun on May 13 by Ephraem Syrus before A.D. 373. [11] In the seventh century Pope Boniface IV introduced the idea into the Western church, in connection with the conversion of the Roman Pantheon into a Christian church, dedicated to the Virgin Mary and all Christian martyrs; the date of May 13 remained. [12] It was perhaps to counteract the popularity of the pagan feast of Samhain that Pope Gregory IV, about A.D. 731, shifted the date to November 1 and broadened the scope to include all saints as well as the martyrs. [13] Some scholars hold, however, that convenience demanded a change, the idea being to take advantage of the availability of harvest crops to feed the hordes of faithful pilgrims descending like locusts on Rome for the feasts of the saints. [14]

In imitation of All Saints' Day, a new celebration, All Souls' Day, was begun (according to tradition) by Saint Odilo, the fifth abbot of Cluny. He decreed about 998 that "all Cluniac monasteries should follow the example of Cluny in offering special prayers and singing the Office for the Dead on the day following the feast of All Saints." [15] Even so, the idea has been traced back as far as the early Middle Ages, especially in Spain, where Pentecost Monday—the seventh Monday after Easter—was dedicated to remembering the dead in the first third of the seventh century. [16] The focus on All Souls' Day is especially upon baptised Christians who are believed to be in purgatory and therefore in special need of prayers on their behalf. [17] As *The New Catholic Encyclopedia* points out,

> throughout the Middle Ages it was popular belief that the souls in purgatory could appear on this day as will-o'-the-wisps, witches, toads, etc., to per-

sons who had wronged them during their life. True Christian concern for the deceased along with superstition were the reasons for the great number of pious foundations for Masses and prayers on their behalf. Many different folkloric and popular customs and practices, especially various forms of food offerings, were associated with All Souls' Day. Among religious traditions, the parish procession to the cemetery, visiting the graves of relatives and friends, and leaving flowers and lights on the graves have remained almost universal. [18]

Thus three recurring details—visits to the graveyard, putting flowers on graves, and the use of lights in connection with the dead—appear in some form in widely separated parts of the world. The celebration of All Souls' Day seems especially to have captured the folk imagination. Christina Hole reports the continued custom of children going "souling" from house to house in some country districts of Cheshire and Shropshire. Somewhat like the trick-or-treaters of recent American Hallowe'en tradition, they sing traditional songs and ask for alms or gifts of fruit or cake. This, says Miss Hole, is all that remains of the custom of asking for soul cake; one of the songs sung in Staffordshire in the eighteenth century included the lines

> Remember the departed for holy Mary's sake,
> And of your charity, pray gi' us a big soul cake. [19]

These soul cakes—*Seelen Brot* in Germany; in Italy, *fave dei morti* ("beans of the dead," referring to the cakes' bean shape); and many other equivalents elsewhere in Europe—are supposed to redeem souls from purgatory. Each cake eaten— or even, by some accounts, each bite—saves a soul. [20]

A holiday atmosphere characterizes Hallowtide, as the period under discussion is often called in England. Church services—masses for the dead—are common in Catholic areas. But throngs of people go to cemeteries in many places with varied results. In Naples in 1888, a writer for the *Satur-day Review* was revolted by the hilarity associated with All Souls' Day and by the Neapolitan custom of keeping the bones of deceased family members around the house. One widower in southern Italy, he related, "has the embalmed corpse of his wife dressed anew once a year in fresh and gorgeous apparel, and seizes the opportunity to present it with a new ring or bracelet."[21]

The use of lights in memorial ways is a special feature of *Yarzeit* services among Jews. Special candles, oil lamps, or even electric light bulbs are burned for twenty-four hours in the home on each anniversary of the death of a loved one, with prayers offered on behalf of the departed. During Rosh Hashanah, customary visits are made to the graves of parents. In formal services four times a year Jewish mourners stand in temple or synagogue while the rabbi names those who have died during the preceding period. Then specific prayers called *Yizkor*—for fathers, mothers, children, or others—are recited by the mourners.[22]

In Puerto Rico, according to one of my students, mourn-ers place lights on graves on All Souls' Day, sometimes can-dles bought with alms begged for that purpose. People cover their heads with burlap as a sign of mourning as they light the candles.[23] The use of candles may be, for the faithful Catho-lic, like the lighting of a votive candle in church; on the other hand, there may be the hint of the concept of a light to guide the spirit of the departed. Here we may recall the origin of the word *funeral*, from the Latin *funus*, for the torch used to guide the departed soul to its eternal abode.[24] Sir James Frazer re-ported the possibility that illumination of homes on one night of the year is related to a commemoration of the death of Osiris.[25]

The celebration of Hallowe'en, the night before All Saints' Day, has become in modern times a period of general hilarity and foolishness, a far cry from the early view that at this sacred time of year spirits of all sorts, especially the wilder ones, were freed for a period ranging from one to three days for a type of homecoming. Thus fires were lit on hilltops in Celtic communities to frighten the witches and evil spirits away.[26] But the availability of spirits at this time led to many games in which the invisible members of the world—even the Devil—helped young people find out who their intended spouses would be, and other divination rituals. "In the north of England," says the chaplain of All Souls' College, Oxford, "October 31 is observed as 'mischief night' marked by tiresome tricks with no serious underlying purpose, meaning, or history."[27]

Following the Reformation, Protestant countries changed the celebration of All Saints' Day to the new dispensation—Reformation Day—commemorating the day Martin Luther "nailed his 95 theses to the door of the castle church in Wittenberg."[28] Even so, the time of year and the commemoration of the dead go on, Protestant or not.

Similar to the Jewish tradition of lighting candles on the anniversary of death, and to the idea of a memorial day common to the whole congregation, is the East Texas custom of holding annual memorial services. The names of those who have died since the previous service are read; a young girl lights a candle as each name is announced. Sandwiches, sodas, and the like are sold to support a custodian for the coming year.[29] In some Mississippi communities, by my own experience, members of a rural church will gather on an appointed day to clear away graveyard weeds and grass, straighten fallen tombstones, and generally make the place presentable. Men and boys usually do the work, and the women and girls bring picnic materials for lunch.[30]

In the Spanish Southwest the European customs related to All Saints' and All Souls' days have merged with the practices of the Indians who preceded the Spanish to the New World. Flowers—especially white ones for children and yellow for adults—were used by the Aztecs to decorate the graves of their loved ones. The flower custom goes on today, with the addition of plastic wreaths, wrought-iron crosses, and crepe paper. People in the more thoroughly Aztec areas of

Simplicity, with a sense of form, marks an humble grave in a desert-land cemetery.

Mexico—Chiapas, Michoacán, and Oaxaca—continue using the special colors, and at least in the 1930s, when Frances Toor described their ways, they were maintaining the custom of evening feasts prepared for the souls visiting them at this sacred time.[31] Half a century ago, family or neighborhood feasts were common in Juárez, Chihuahua, but times there are changing.[32] Still, *pan de muertos* ("bread for the dead" or soul bread) is prepared annually by bakers. Made in huge round loaves with the shape of bones on top, and decorated with purple sugar, the bread is almost as sweet as cake, and is eaten eagerly—but with no thought of saving souls from purgatory, at least for those I have interviewed.

Spun sugar skulls with sequined eyes are still bought to give to one's friends, with the recipient's name on the forehead. In metropolitan Mexico City presents in the shape of miniature coffins with skeletons inside are given to children. Despite these macabre (to foreigners) touches, All Saints' Day is often called *Día de los Angelitos* ("Day of the Little Angels"), reflecting the early development of the day to include infants among the saints and martyrs.

Poems something like comic valentines are sold on the street, in Mexico City and elsewhere, to send to friend or foe, poking fun at their foibles or their politics, but always ending with the observation that all this doesn't matter anyway, since the person under discussion is a *calavera* ("skull") and is already dead.[33]

After breakfast, and perhaps a visit to the neighborhood church, where a candle is lighted in memory of departed family members, the people of Juárez descend, literally by the thousands, upon the marketplace to buy flowers (real or plastic), wreaths (called *coronas*, or "crowns"), crosses, or some work of colorful art to decorate the graves of their loved ones. Brightly painted wreaths made of tin are popular, as are a host of other items that artisans have worked for days to prepare for this holiday. Shops that sell such everyday items as herbs or beans or clay pots bring out the plastic flower wreaths left over from the year before and dust them off for sale. Some lucky people have flowers from their own yards, especially marigolds and chrysanthemums, to take to their loved ones.

By car, by bus, or on foot—some walking for many miles—people converge on the cemetery. The flower vendors have preceded them, setting up shop at the gates with other vendors who sell tacos, tamales, soft drinks, and sweets of many kinds. Sugar cane (*caña*) is in season, and many a set of teeth is busy stripping off the outside to get at the juicy pulp within.

All Souls' or All Saints' Day—it matters little what the actual date is—cannot be considered complete by most of the faithful without a visit to the cemetery. When the first and

Twisted crepe paper adorns a grave which has been lovingly decorated by surviving family members, who were quite proud of their artistry.

second of November fall on a weekend, the entire weekend finds the cemeteries crowded with people. If the special days are during the week, people who cannot leave their work come when they can. I have known working maids, for whom the daily wage is essential to survival, to come to the grave-yard after a ten- or twelve-hour day to do their duty to those members of the family who have gone before. Some even take the day off, at considerable sacrifice, to fulfill this sacred obligation. Although the merging of the dates is common, even for the church, the folk tend to hold on to tradition to a considerable degree. For instance, in 1980 All Saints' Day fell on a Saturday, and I was surprised at the relatively small amount of activity when we went to the cemetery in the after-noon. Everyone I asked replied, "Wait till tomorrow; *that* is All Souls' Day." And almost invariably, those I observed were tending to the graves of *Angelitos,* as was proper for the date.

Tepeyac Panteón in Juárez, where I have visited with my family each year for over a decade, is a typical Mexican graveyard. There is no fund for perpetual maintenance, and the majority of the families do their own grave tending personally. Poor and not so poor, they gather by the thousands to do their duty and to visit with their dead. Hordes of youngsters, armed with brooms, hoes, rakes, and the indispensable plastic jug, are available to help out in the annual process of pulling weeds, piling up mounds of dirt on the poorer graves, and freshening the earth and the flowers with water carried from the sparsely provided water faucets in the cemetery.

Side by side with a family prayer session at graveside may be a picnic; no apparent lack of respect is involved. Although the religious nature of the time is plain, I have never seen a priest in religious garb in Tepeyac cemetery. Of course, since the Mexican Revolution it is against the law for priests to appear in public in their clerical robes,[34] so it may be that priests *not* in uniform have been there all the time.

A neglected grave usually means that there is no living or able-bodied relative left to take on the family responsibility. Some grave markers, especially the crosses made of simple two-by-fours, blasted by sun and sandstorm, may carry only a single flower, or even a twisted bit of paper ribbon salvaged from somebody's decorated package. Some of the grave decorations I have seen have not been altered in years—the same faded bow bearing mute testimony that there is nobody left to care for that grave.

The young members of the family learn how to do their duty by watching or by taking part in the cleaning and decorating of graves. It may be that the calm acceptance of death so many sociologists find among Mexicans stems in part from this early annual reminder received by children that death is all around us, and it is nothing to be feared. The relaxed picnic quality of the activity certainly suggests that for the Mexican, death is less fearful than in some other cultures.

One student of folk custom, in a book intended for visitors to the 1968 Olympic games, made the following sweeping statement about the national character:

Mexicans are fascinated by the macabre, and death means little to them. Their attitude goes back to the Inquisition and their ancestors' pagan faith. Human sacrifices then formed one of the central features of their worship and there were days on which, literally, countless men and women were offered to the rain-god or deity of fertility. This feeling toward death has really never changed. No wonder that today Mexican undertakers display in show-windows a whole section of coffins. It is a sight which doesn't offend passersby. In the light of all this it is not surprising that one of the most popular festivals of Mexican Christians is the Day

While mother and child decorate the grave mound, the wooden cross gets a fresh paint job and a hand-lettered name.

of the Dead, celebrated on November 2nd. The people look upon it as a happy, annual time of reunion with the spirits of the departed. Certainly in Mexico's celebration of the Day of the Dead death has lost its sting and the voice of weeping changes into the sound of laughter.[35]

I am more inclined to feel that a realistic acceptance of death as a universal is at work here, not some fascination with the macabre. In fact, there is a Mexican folktale in which Jesus or God is turned away when he comes begging at a poor Mexican's door, but *La Muerte*—Death—is welcomed: He treats rich and poor alike.[36]

While a carved marble headstone may adorn one gravesite in Tepeyac cemetery, nearby a family may intensify the lettering scratched into a cement headstone by applying red or gold paint, or a wooden cross may be made fresh and new with painstaking care. The curbing around a grave might be mended with a mixture of cement and sand brought from home in a paper sack and prepared by hand on the site. The contrast between rich and poor is strong here. The rich family may have a marbled floor set apart by a tall iron fence, with flowers obviously prepared by floral designers. Even so, there is a sense of form and proportion often evident in the decorations on the humblest graves.

The desolation inherent in cemeteries—especially in the wind-swept, barren, and rock landscape of the Southwest—is dispelled to a large degree by the family devotion spent so lovingly on All Saints' and All Souls' days. The lack of strict observance of the differences between the days, and the blending of practices some would call pagan with those encouraged by formal religion, together with the picnics and holiday atmosphere, all speak of the changes going on in the long-standing tradition of All Saints' and All Souls' days. But the customs are alive in the Spanish Southwest, and they are not likely to die away so long as life itself goes on here.

A carefully shaped mound with a single flower, showing family concern, is next to a floral spray done professionally.

Notes

1. *El Paso, Texas, Times,* 31 October 1974.
2. "All Souls' Day," *The New Catholic Encyclopedia,* 1967 ed.
3. William S. Walsh, *Curiosities of Popular Customs* (Philadelphia: Lippincott, 1898), p. 29.
4. Ibid.
5. "Lunar New Year, Chinese," *World Almanac* (New York: Newspaper Enterprise Association, 1981), p. 787; Mary Tachibana, interview, El Paso, Texas, 15 September 1980.
6. Ensho Ashikaga, "The Festival for the Spirits of the Dead," *Western Folklore* 9 (1950): 217.
7. Tachibana interview.

8. Ashikaga, "Festival," p. 218; also Rudolph Brasch, *How Did It Begin?* (New York: David McKay, 1967), pp. 60–61.
9. Walsh, *Curiosities*, p. 29; also Christina Hole, *British Customs* (London: Hutchinson, 1976), p. 188. John E. P. Mullally of Eastern Illinois University, serious student of Gaelic, warns that many scholars have erroneously assumed that Samhain was a god, which simply isn't so. Personal correspondence, 3 April 1986.
10. Jane Hatch, *The American Book of Days*, 3rd ed. (New York: H. W. Wilson, 1978), p. 968.
11. "All Saints, Festival of," *Encyclopaedia Britannica*, 1973 ed.
12. Walsh, *Curiosities*, p. 28.
13. Ibid.; "All Saints, Festival of," *Encyclopaedia Britannica*.
14. Hatch, *American Book of Days*, p. 979; also "All Saints, Feast of," *The New Catholic Encyclopedia*.
15. "All Souls' Day," *The New Catholic Encyclopedia*; see also Hatch, *American Book of Days*, p. 980.
16. "All Souls' Day," *The New Catholic Encyclopedia*.
17. Hatch, *American Book of Days*, p. 980; Hole, *British Customs*, p. 188.
18. "All Souls' Day," *The New Catholic Encyclopedia*.
19. Hole, *British Customs*, pp. 187–88.
20. Ibid., p. 188; Hatch, *American Book of Days*, p. 981; also reports of various folklore students at the University of Texas at El Paso who have lived in foreign countries in recent years.
21. Walsh, *Curiosities*, pp. 31–32, citing *Saturday Review*, 7 January 1888.
22. Miriam Reisel Gladstein, interview, El Paso, Texas, 20 September 1980; Deborah M. Melamed, *The Three Pillars: Thought, Worship and Practice for the Jewish Woman* (New York: Women's League of the United Synagogue of America, 1927), pp. 93, 149–54.
23. Felix Rubert-Negron, a folklore student at the University of Texas at El Paso, interview, 21 September 1980. He was born and lived until the age of twenty-five in Puerto Rico.
24. Brasch, *How Did It Begin?*, pp. 60–61.
25. James G. Frazer, *The New Golden Bough*, ed. Theodor H. Gaster (New York: Criterion Books, 1959), p. 334. Frazer also cites numerous All Souls' types of celebrations (pp. 334–37).
26. Hatch, *American Book of Days*, pp. 968–69.
27. Rev. Edwin Oliver James, "Halloween," *Encyclopaedia Britannica*.
28. Hatch, *American Book of Days*, p. 974; see also "All Souls' Day," *Encyclopaedia Britannica*.
29. Robert Cowser, "Community Memorial Day Observances in Northeast Texas," *Western Folklore* 31 (1972): 120–21.

30. A similar custom is described by Guy Kirtley in "'Hoping Out' in East Texas," in J. Frank Dobie, Mody C. Boatright, and Harry H. Ransom, eds., *Texian Stomping Grounds*, PTFS XVII (Austin: Texas Folklore Society, 1941; reprint, Dallas: Southern Methodist University Press, 1967), p. 32.

31. Frances Toor, *A Treasury of Mexican Folkways* (New York: Crown Publishers, 1947), pp. 236–44.

32. Lucina Lara Rey de Fischer, interview, El Paso, Texas, 31 October 1974.

33. Jovita Varela, director of the Juárez Museo de Arte e Historia, in an interview with folklore student Luz Taboada, 2 November 1977. *Calaveras* (skulls) were often featured in the related political cartoons of José Guadalupe Posada, famed Mexican artist-engraver; see Ron Tyler, ed., *Posada's Mexico* (Washington, D.C.: The Library of Congress in cooperation with the Amon Carter Museum of Art, 1979). See also Paul Westheim, *La Calavera*, trans. Mariana Frank, 2nd ed. (Mexico, D.F.: Ediciones Era, 1971); Toor, *Treasury of Mexican Folkways*, pp. 237–38.

34. On June 14, 1926, President Plutarco Elías Calles of Mexico published the "Ley Calles," a strict enforcement of the anti-clerical elements of the constitution of 1917. Article 18 prescribed a fine of 500 pesos or fifteen days in jail for anyone appearing in public in any form of distinctive clerical garb—even the priestly collar. See Joseph H. L. Schlarman, *Mexico: A Land of Volcanoes*, 2nd ed. (Milwaukee: Bruce Publishing Co., 1950), pp. 501–2.

35. Rudolph Brasch, *Mexico: A Country of Contrasts* (New York: David McKay, 1967), p. 124. A more restrained view is that of Ken Flynn, from the *El Paso Herald-Post*, 28 October 1978.

36. The story is widely collected in the Spanish Southwest. See Stanley L. Robe, *Hispanic Folktales from New Mexico*, Folklore Studies 30 (Berkeley and Los Angeles: University of California Press, 1977), pp. 78–80; also Honora DeBusk Smith, "Mexican Plazas Along the River of Souls," in J. Frank Dobie, ed., *Southwestern Lore*, PTFS IX (Austin: Texas Folklore Society, 1931; reprint, Dallas: Southern Methodist University Press, 1965), pp. 70–71.

All photographs reproduced by permission of John O. West.

One of the two lime kilns on the Ochoa Ranch, which produced much of the lime used in the silver mines at Shafter around the turn of the century. These kilns were used for many years and were occasionally relined with adobe bricks.

JOE S. GRAHAM

Mexican-American Lime Kilns in West Texas
The Limits of Folk Technology

LIME-MAKING has been a part of the Hispanic culture in the Big Bend of West Texas for centuries, brought into the area by early Spanish soldiers and clerics. It persisted as an active part of the folk tradition until early in this century, and while one can still find old abandoned *caleras* (lime kilns) along the Rio Grande in the Big Bend, they have not been used for decades. This paper has a twofold purpose: First, to describe the lime-making process used by Mexican Americans in the Big Bend of West Texas and to note its importance in the culture; and second, to attempt to explain why lime-making, like many other folk technologies, disappeared.

Lime Production: A Brief History

Lime is one of man's oldest chemicals, and its use as a cementing and plastering material is almost as old as the history of fire.[1] Archaeologists have discovered primitive lime kilns dating to the Stone Age. Robert S. Boynton notes that lime found many uses in early historic times as well: the Egyptians used it as a mortar and plaster in their pyramids between 4000 and 2000 B.C.; although lime was used mainly in construction, the Greek and early Roman empires used it as a chemical for bleaching; the Romans used saturated solutions

73

of lime water as medicine in the first century A.D.; the first great highway builders, the Romans, used limestone and lime extensively; one of the early forms of chemical warfare involved the English practice of throwing quicklime into the faces of the French during their war of 1217.[2] The processes for making and using lime were passed from civilization to civilization, becoming common throughout Europe by the time of the discovery of America. In spite of the ubiquity of lime in the civilized world, lime processing remained almost unchanged until the early 1900s, with most of the changes occurring after 1935.[3]

Even in pre-Hispanic America, through independent discovery or cultural diffusion, the Incas and the Mayas mastered the art of making lime mortars which would last for centuries. Some of the ancient buildings have stood for two or three thousand years, and restoration societies have discovered that the scientifically prepared mortars used in the restoration process may have to be renewed in five to twenty years.[4]

On the East Coast of the United States, the British introduced the processes for making and using lime. Quicklime was produced locally in Rhode Island as early as 1635, but it was not until 1733, when boatloads of lime were shipped from Rockland, Maine, to Boston, that lime manufacturing emerged as a significant commercial industry.[5] The commercial slaking (hydration) of lime began in the early twentieth century.

On the other side of the continent, almost a century earlier, the Spaniards brought the lime-production processes to the New World and ensured their spread throughout the Spanish empire. Lime and its production and use are a part of the Spanish legacy to the Southwest, even though, as noted above, lime and lime mortars were used by the Incas and Mayas.

Cal (Lime) in La Junta: A Spanish Introduction

Archaeological and historical evidence makes it clear

that the Spaniards did indeed introduce lime (*cal*) and its many uses to La Junta (now Ojinaga, Chihuahua, Mexico, and Presidio, Texas) and other areas of the Southwest. Let us briefly examine this evidence. Although there is some difference of opinion as to the chronology of the pre-Hispanic peoples indigenous to the La Junta area, a general outline of the different tribes and their chronology will suffice. Howard Applegate and Wayne Hanselka claim that this area seems to encompass "the oldest continuously cultivated farms in the United States."[6] The earliest inhabitants, apparently related to the southern Arizona Cochise, date back to about 1500 B.C. Sometime around 900 A.D., the Mogollon-Anasazi moved into the area, only to be replaced by a number of different tribes between this time and the arrival of the first Europeans, who were to discover the Patarabueyes (Julimes), the Jumanos, and a number of smaller tribes living in the area.

Archaeologists who have studied these groups have discovered no evidence of the use of lime mortar or plaster in the cave dwellings or pithouses of prehistoric groups in the area. While both John Kelley and W. J. Shackleford report the use of mud plaster in the early pithouses of Redford and surrounding areas, there was no evidence of the use of lime.[7] Records of early Spanish *entradas* verify the absence of lime. Pedro de Castañeda, a private soldier who traveled with the Coronado expedition into New Mexico, described the process of house construction among the Indians at Tiguex, a province of about twelve villages on the banks of the Rio Grande near Taos, New Mexico.

> They all work together to build the villages, the women being engaged in making the mixture and the walls, while the men bring the wood and put it in place. They have no lime, but they make a mixture of ashes, coals, and dirt which is almost as good as mortar, for when the house is to have four stories, they do not make the walls more than half a yard thick. They gather a great pile of thyme [sagebrush] and sedge grass and set it afire, and when it is

half coals and ashes they throw a quantity of dirt and water on it and mix it all together. They make round balls of this, which they use instead of stones after they dry, fixing them with the same mixture, which comes to be like a stiff clay.[8]

It is clear from archaeological evidence that the pre-Hispanic inhabitants of La Junta did not make and use lime.

Burning Lime in the Big Bend

While lime is no longer burned in the La Junta area, it was once a thriving industry. Its chemical properties made it very important to the early inhabitants of the region, in fact allowed them to more effectively exploit certain elements of their physical environment. To understand just how important lime was to them, we must examine the many ways it was used by the Mexicans and Mexican Americans of the region.

Lime was essential to the processing of the most basic staple in the diet—corn. The hard kernels of corn must be processed before humans can eat them. One can simply grind them into corn meal, as Anglos have done, but this was a time-consuming task at best, and practically impossible without a grist mill. The corn can be toasted and then ground into a fine powder, a practice used both by the Indians and Mexicans. *Pinole* (made from toasted, ground corn flavored with cinnamon or other flavor and sweetened with sugar or *piloncillo,* the crude unrefined sugar common in the area) and *atole* (made from finely ground parched corn mixed with milk—goat's or cow's—or water and flavored and sweetened as a breakfast cereal) are two dishes which predate the Spaniards in the area.[9] Both have Nahuatl names.

By far the most common method of preparing dried corn, however, requires lime. One places the corn in a container, adds water and a bit of lime, and cooks it for a few hours. The caustic lime dissolves the hard shell on the corn, leaving a hominy-like cooked kernel. Anglos and blacks in the South, of course, used lye to achieve the same purpose—but its use is unknown in this area. After the corn is rinsed a few times, the softened kernel may then be ground on a metate or in a small hand mill, both as essential to pioneer life as blenders and microwaves are to the modern kitchen. If it is to be used for tamales, the corn is ground into a fairly coarse paste called *nixtamal*; if it is to be used for tortillas, it is ground into a very fine paste called *masa*. The kernels may be eaten whole, like hominy, in a dish called *pozole* (fr. Nahuatl), a spicy meat broth often eaten for breakfast, or in *menudo* (beef tripe stew), a dish known to most Texans. Whatever the final use, the corn must first be processed with lime, and though not much lime is actually used in the process, it is nevertheless vital to that process. The lime which remains in the corn after the rinsing was an important source of calcium for these people, who had few other sources of this important mineral in their diets (they drank little milk).

The vast majority of the lime processed in the La Junta area was used in construction of one kind or another. Lime, used as a plaster and as a mortar, was the cement of the time—one has only to imagine our own society without concrete. It was used not only in building houses, but also in building dams, irrigation canals, gravestones and covers, and especially in the silver mines in Shafter and the quicksilver mines in Terlingua. One of the earliest and most important uses of lime was in the construction of dwellings, a practice brought to the New World by the Spaniards.

While adobe houses do not require lime to the same degree that stone houses do, lime can make the difference between having just a liveable shelter or a comfortable home. Mexicans and Mexican Americans in West Texas used the *mezcla de cal y arena* (lime and sand mortar) in house construction far less than their counterparts in South Texas, from Laredo down to Brownsville. In the Big Bend area, I have photographed and documented a number of *jacales* (small, one-room houses indigenous to the area, consisting of a roof

supported by four forked corner posts buried a foot or so in the
ground, with walls of smaller limbs or of ocotillo, plastered
with mud inside and out), and only one of them was plastered
on the outside with the *mezcla de cal y arena*. Ada K. Newton,
on the other hand, reports that the *jacales* in South Texas were
commonly plastered with this *enjarre* (plaster)—a practice I
also documented in the palisade *jacales* in Brackettville.[10]

While few of the *albañiles* (masons/carpenters) in the Big
Bend area are old enough to have used *enjarre* on the adobe
houses they built—cement had become common by the time
most had begun their trade—a number of the older houses in
Mulatto, Redford, Presidio, Ojinaga, El Indio, Ruidoso, Can-
delaria, and on the old Ochoa Ranch outside of Presidio were
plastered with the *enjarre de cal y arena*. The finer homes of
the well-to-do were most often graced with such a coating.
Carmen Orozco, an *albañil* from Redford and Presidio, remembers seeing as a child how the *enjarre de cal y arena* was
made. He described a process very similar to that recorded by
José Roberto Juarez, Jr., in a study done for the Ranching
Heritage Center at Texas Tech.

> . . . store-bought lime was used in Papa Kike's time
> [ca. 1914, when the last house in Dolores, Texas,
> was built—Papa Kike, Juarez's grandfather, helped
> build it] to make a lime enjarre that was just as
> strong as cement. This mezcla (mixture) was made
> in a cajon (box) that measured about $1' \times 5'$. This
> cajon was called a mezclera. The sand and lime
> were mixed well in this box and then formed into a
> cone (cone-shaped pile) on the floor. This cone
> was left for a period of time ranging from a few days
> to five weeks. This would apagar (slake) the mix-
> ture. Whenever the mezcla was needed, water was
> added to make it manageable and it could then be
> easily spread with a cuchara (trowel). The fact that
> the mezcla could be left for weeks at a time with no
> ill effects gave it a major advantage over cement.

Cement can only be wet once and must be used immediately. Mezcla, however, could be made and used at one's convenience.[11]

Orozco claims that leaving the *mezcla* to sit awhile actually improved the quality of the plaster.

Lime-Making: The Folk Process

The lime used in the Big Bend was processed in kilns located in the sides of hills or dry arroyos. The raw material, limestone, is common in the area, both in the form of round stones of varying sizes and in layered formations which can be quarried. I have identified some twenty-seven kilns in the region, large and small. The largest is about eight to nine feet in diameter and about twenty-five feet deep—it would burn several tons of lime at a time. The typical kiln is about five to six feet in diameter and perhaps eight feet deep. Kilns are dug into the side of a steep hill so that the walls will be thin enough on one side to permit the digging of a tunnel (around two feet in diameter) from the outside into the bottom of the kiln. This tunnel is used to feed the fire and to remove the ashes.

The limestone is brought in and carefully stacked in the kiln, leaving a dome-like space four or five feet high at the bottom, a fire space called the *bóveda*. The selection and stacking of this rock requires great skill, if the burn is to be successful. Prior to placing these stones in the kiln, the *caleros* must gather from four to six thousand *manojos* (bundles) of *guame* (greasewood), a plant which grows abundantly in the area and which burns with an extremely high heat. Each *manojo* is ten to twelve inches in diameter. Once the fuel is collected and the stones are in place, the burning is begun. Once started, the fire must be maintained constantly for three days and three nights. When the smoke emerging from the top of the kiln is white, the lime is cooked and the fire is permitted to die. Once cooled, the stones—now quicklime—

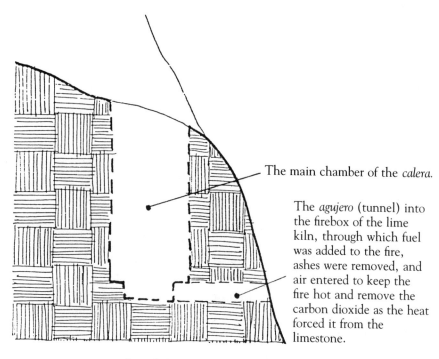

The main chamber of the *calera*.

The *agujero* (tunnel) into the firebox of the lime kiln, through which fuel was added to the fire, ashes were removed, and air entered to keep the fire hot and remove the carbon dioxide as the heat forced it from the limestone.

Lime kilns were placed in the side of low hills.

are removed and prepared for slaking. They are first ground into a fine powder—a relatively easy task, since a few drops of water sprinkled on a "stone" of quicklime causes a violent reaction, like a very small explosion, turning the stone to a fine powder.

The quicklime is extremely caustic and unstable and must be slaked (hydrated) before it can be used. Slaking consists of mixing water with the quicklime and letting it set. Once dried, the slaked lime is ground into powder and sold for use in any number of applications.

Lime-Making Disappears,
A Victim of Modern Technology

It should be noted that competition by commercially produced lime began some time before other products—especially portland cement—began replacing locally produced lime. Although commercial lime was available in stores by the turn of the century, local lime production continued in the area until the 1940s. And while lime is still used in processing corn at home, portland cement has replaced it in most construction applications. The only lime available today is commercially produced. The remainder of this paper will attempt to explain why commercially produced lime replaced the lime made by the *caleros,* who once provided it for everyone in the region. I shall argue that the folk technology disappeared principally because it could not compete economically with commercial science-based technology; that is, one could buy lime more cheaply at the store than from the *calero.* While we recognize adaptability as one of the more important characteristics of folklore, this folk technology had become as economically efficient as the folk craftsmen could make it, given the kind of knowledge they had about the process. This folk technology, like others, disappeared in great measure because it could not adapt sufficiently to compete with science-based technology. And it could not adapt precisely because of the *kind* of knowledge it was based upon.

Few scholars have seriously inquired into the differences between science-based technology, common in our mainstream culture in the United States, and folk technology, which is based on a different kind or order of knowledge and which asks different kinds of questions. One exception is Claude Lévi-Strauss, who has argued in *The Savage Mind* that Neolithic man was heir to a long scientific tradition—how could he otherwise have discovered the process of smelting copper, which could not have been accidental? Or how could he have learned to make stout, waterproof, kiln-fired clay vessels, or learned to cultivate crops? These achievements "required a genuinely scientific attitude, sustained and watchful interest and a desire for knowledge for its own sake," yet between the "Neolithic revolution" and modern science were centuries of stagnation, "like a level plain between ascents." [12] Why? Lévi-Strauss explains the paradox by postulating that

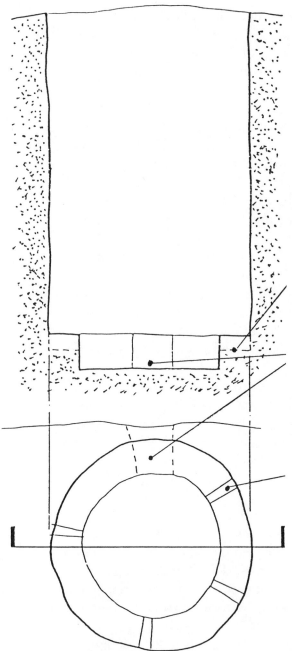

Though there was considerable variation in size, the typical kiln was five to six feet in diameter and eight to ten feet deep.

At the bottom of the kiln is a small shelf of dirt upon which the base of the *bóveda* (a dome-like hollow space in the stacked limestone) rested.

The *agujero* (small tunnel) leading from the firebox in the bottom of the kiln to the outside—used for adding fuel and removing ashes.

The *lumbrero* (a small trench cut in the shelf supporting the *bóveda*) carried fire and heat to the outside edge of the kiln to insure a complete burn throughout.

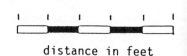

distance in feet

Drawing by Eric Connell.

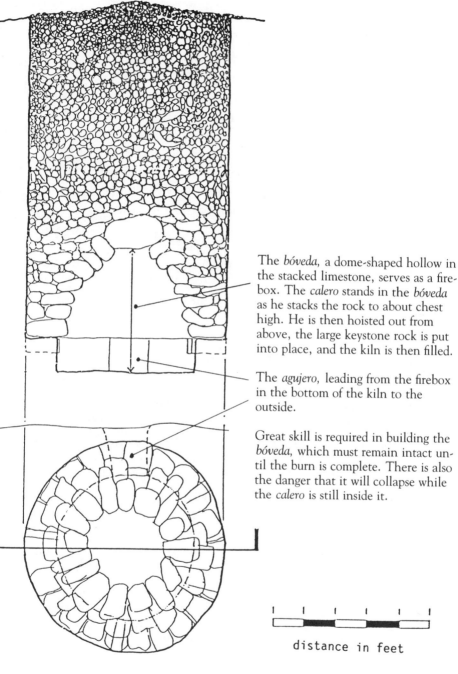

The *bóveda*, a dome-shaped hollow in the stacked limestone, serves as a fire-box. The *calero* stands in the *bóveda* as he stacks the rock to about chest high. He is then hoisted out from above, the large keystone rock is put into place, and the kiln is then filled.

The *agujero*, leading from the firebox in the bottom of the kiln to the outside.

Great skill is required in building the *bóveda*, which must remain intact until the burn is complete. There is also the danger that it will collapse while the *calero* is still inside it.

distance in feet

Drawing by Eric Connell.

Mexican-American Lime Kilns · 83

there are two distinct modes of scientific thought. They are, he argues,

> not a function of different stages of development of the human mind but rather of two strategic levels at which nature is accessible to scientific enquiry: one roughly adapted to that of perception and the imagination: the other at a remove from it. It is as if the necessary connections which are the object of all science, neolithic or modern, could be arrived at by two different routes, one very close to, and the other more remote from, sensible intuition.[13]

This "science of the concrete," as he calls it,

> was necessarily restricted by its essence to results other than those destined to be achieved by the exact natural sciences but it was no less scientific and its results no less genuine. They were secured ten thousand years earlier and still remain at the basis of our own civilization.[14]

In our society, technology is based on scientific discoveries. Engineers, for example, apply the principles discovered by physicists to design and build bridges and buildings. The modern conveniences which we depend upon for our leisure and even our very existence—from television to X-ray machines to Cat-Scan machines—are firmly based in scientific principles understood by the designer and builder of these modern marvels, though likely not understood by those using them.

Folk technology, on the other hand, is based in empirically discovered processes—trial and error experiments and observations—not in an understanding of the principles of chemistry, physics, or cellular biology. For example, the M.D. understands how streptococcus bacteria cause strep throat and how penicillin attacks and destroys bacteria cells without harming the host animal cells. On the other hand, the folk healer, while he or she has a general theory about the causes of such a folk illness as *mal de ojo* and knows the appropriate remedy for it, does not have the same kind of precise knowledge as to *why* the remedy works—what the specific mechanism is. That is not to denigrate folk medicine or to say that the folk treatments do not work, for many of them do. It is simply to say that the knowledge base is different. Consequently, folk technology has limitations which do not exist with science-based technology.

Lime-Making: A Chemical Process

Making lime from limestone is perhaps the simplest kind of chemical reaction—thermal decomposition. Although man has made lime since Neolithic times, it wasn't until the nineteenth century that French scientists recorded the earliest fundamental data and identified the dissociation temperature and pressure incident to turning limestone into lime, as well as evaluated structural limes and mortars for construction. In spite of the ubiquity of lime in the civilized world, lime processing remained almost unchanged until the early twentieth century.[15] Let us briefly examine what happens when limestone is heated or "burned" to produce lime.

First of all, limestone is a very stable element.[16] That is, it will change very slowly, if at all, under normal conditions. The burning process produces quicklime, which is far less stable and is quite vulnerable to moisture. When quicklime is slaked, or hydrated, it becomes more stable, and water will not further alter its composition.

The chemical process in lime production is quite simple. Briefly, one hundred molecules of high-calcium limestone ($CaCO_3$), when heated to a high enough temperature ($1700°$–$2450°$ F) for a long enough period of time (depending on stone size, from a few hours to as many as three days or longer) will produce fifty-six molecules of high-calcium quicklime (CaO) and forty-four molecules of carbon dioxide (CO_2). The chemical formula looks like this:

$$(100)CaCO_3 + heat \rightleftharpoons (56)CaO + (44)CO_2$$

When lime is burned, it loses about 44 percent of its weight as

This handsome watering trough, located on a ranch near San Carlos in northern Chihuahua, is made of lime, sand, and gravel.

the CO_2 dissipates. However, the quicklime, when exposed for a time to carbon dioxide, can revert back to a limestone form, giving off heat in the process. The process is slow and the heat is seldom intense.

Most of the lime used for construction purposes is slaked,

or hydrated. In slaking, eighteen molecules of water (H_2O), when added to fifty-six molecules of quicklime (CaO), produce seventy-four molecules of slaked lime, or high-calcium hydrate [Ca(OH)$_2$], generating enough heat in the process to become very warm to the touch. The chemical formula for this reaction is as follows:

$$(56)CaO + (18)H_2O \rightarrow (74)Ca(OH)_2 + heat$$

Slaked lime, when heated enough, reverts back to quicklime:

$$(74)Ca(OH)_2 + heat \rightarrow (56)CaO + H_2O \text{ (water vapor)}$$

It should be noted that both quicklime and slaked lime can be dangerous to work with. A very caustic base, lime can blind a person if it gets into his eyes, can burn his skin with prolonged contact, and can damage his nose, throat, and lungs if breathed in powder form. This caustic nature makes it useful in the processing of *nixtamal* or *masa* from hard-shelled, dry corn.

One further bit of information will help us to better understand how lime works in construction applications: that is, why (or how) does it work? How does it do what it does? According to A. B. Searle, the process is quite simple. In lime mortar, the lime forms a gel with the water in the mixture, and this gel coats the sand grains. As the mortar dries, the gel dries and shrinks, holding the sand grains together. The interlacing of the crystals of the calcium carbonate increases the strength of the mass.[17]

One reason portland cement has replaced lime mortar in many applications is that cement is harder and stronger, a fact which also comes from the nature of lime. Again, as Searle explains it, mortar made with lime does not "set" in the same manner as concrete. It merely dries, and by gradually absorbing carbon dioxide on its surface, becomes moderately hard (about like limestone) externally, but the interior mass may remain soft for several hundred years.[18] This characteristic makes lime ideal for plastering adobe structures. The lime mortar expands and contracts without cracking. Plaster made of portland cement, on the other hand, tends to crack under the kinds of temperature changes common in West Texas. Once the cement plaster cracks, rain water enters the cracks and washes the adobe material away, eventually destroying the structure. I have photographed a number of adobe houses in the Big Bend with roofs plastered with cement. When the cracks occurred, the house owners have used tar to repair the cracks—a practice which is not always effective. The Texas Historical Commission strongly recommends *not* using portland cement in repairing historic adobe structures.

As Searle, Boynton, and others have noted, there are four essential requirements to producing good lime from limestone: (1) it is necessary to use a suitable limestone; (2) it is necessary to heat the limestone to the temperature necessary to decompose it into lime (but overheating will ruin the lime)—the proper fuel is necessary; (3) the limestone must be kept at this temperature long enough for the decomposition process to be completed; and (4) the carbon dioxide produced in the chemical reaction must be removed as quickly as possible.[19]

The Mexican-American and Mexican *caleros* of the La Junta area—using their considerable knowledge and skill in building a successful updraft kiln (in contrast to the modern rotary kiln) and in selecting, stacking, and firing the limestone—were able to meet these requirements. Though they had no knowledge of the chemical composition of limestone or of what kinds of impurities it might contain, they knew from experience what local limestone made the best lime. Though they did not know the critical dissociation temperature of limestone, they knew that *guame* produced a high enough heat to make good lime. They also knew that they had to keep the fire stoked for three days and nights to get a good burn. And finally, although they did not understand that the carbon dioxide must be quickly removed as it escaped from the limestone, they knew that the top of the kiln must remain open for the updraft to carry the heat up through the stones. So they were able to make good lime not through an

Graves in the cemetery at the Ochoa Ranch near Presidio. The center grave dates to the turn of the century.

understanding of the chemical processes, but by the process we call folklore—traditional knowledge, passed from generation to generation through word of mouth, used to meet recurring problems and needs in a culture.

Conclusion

The Mexican Americans of West Texas made their own lime and used it in many forms, as did their Spanish and Mexican ancestors before them. They did not understand the chemical processes which would transform limestone into quicklime and then into slaked lime to be used in food processing and construction. They simply relied on tradition—on the folk process—to learn to make and use this valuable chemical. And they used it quite effectively to enhance their way of life. However, local lime production diminished rapidly around the turn of the century because lime could be commercially produced and sold for less than the local *caleros* were willing to accept. Products like portland cement have also reduced the demand for lime.

Like much folk technology, traditional lime-making has disappeared because it could not compete with modern science-based technology. Using the knowledge of chemistry and physics, man has been able to design lime kilns which produce large quantities of lime quickly and inexpensively. Folk technology allowed early inhabitants to exploit their environment quite effectively, but there was no way to improve the process and make it more efficient without understanding the chemistry of the process of transforming limestone to lime. While commercially produced lime is no better than that produced through the folk process, and some would argue that it is not as good, the folk process was not efficient enough to survive. Other folk technologies have disappeared, and others are now disappearing because they, too, can no longer compete.

All photographs reproduced by permission of Joe Graham.

Notes

1. Raymond Kirk and Donald F. Othmer, *Encyclopedia of Chemical Technology*, 3rd ed. (New York: John Wiley & Sons, 1967), p. 419.
2. Robert S. Boynton, *Chemistry and Technology of Lime and Limestone* (New York: John Wiley & Sons, 1966), p. 3.
3. Ibid., p. 204.
4. Ibid., p. 4.
5. Kirk and Othmer, *Chemical Technology*, p. 419.
6. Howard G. Applegate and C. Wayne Hanselka, *La Junta de Los Ríos del Norte y Conchos* (El Paso: Texas Western Press, 1974), p. 4.
7. John C. Kelley, "The Historic Indian Pueblos of La Junta de los Ríos, I," *New Mexico Historical Review* 27 (1952): 21–51; W. J. Shackleford, "Excavation at the Polvo Site in Western Texas," *American Antiquity* 20 (1955): 256–62.
8. Pedro de Castañeda, "The Narrative of the Expedition of Coronado by Castaneda," in Frederick W. Hodge, ed. and trans., *Spanish Explorers in the Southern United States, 1528–1543* (New York: Scribners, 1907), pp. 352–53.
9. Joe S. Graham, "Foodways of Pioneer Texas-Mexicans," in LeRoy Johnson, Jr., ed., *Texana I* (Austin: Texas Historical Commission, 1983).
10. Ada K. Newton, "The History of Architecture along the Rio Grande as Reflected in the Buildings around Rio Grande City 1749–1920" (Masters thesis, Texas A&I University, Kingsville, 1964).
11. José Roberto Juarez, Jr., "An Architectural Description of Dolores Ranch" (manuscript, Ranching Heritage Center, Texas Tech Museum, Lubbock, Texas, 1976), pp. 6–7.
12. Claude Lévi-Strauss, *The Savage Mind* (Chicago: University of Chicago Press, 1966), pp. 14–15.
13. Ibid., p. 15.
14. Ibid., p. 16.
15. Boynton, *Lime and Limestone*, p. 204.
16. Kirk and Othmer, *Chemical Technology*, p. 429.
17. A. B. Searle, *Limestone and Its Products* (London: E. Benn, Ltd., 1935), p. 270.
18. Ibid.
19. Ibid.; Boynton, *Lime and Limestone*.

Texon Oil & Land Company's Santa Rita No. 1, University Lands, Reagan County, Texas, 1923. *From the San Angelo Standard Times Collection.*

EDWARD C. ROWLAND

A Rose Blooms in the Desert

The Saga of the Santa Rita # 1

After the discovery in 1901 of immense amounts of oil on the Texas gulf coast, oilmen began searching elsewhere across the state. Despite encouraging signs, the vast area of West Texas soon earned a reputation as an "oilman's graveyard." That image still held when Captain Rupert Ricker returned from World War I to hang his lawyer's shingle in the small town of San Angelo.

Ricker spent his ample spare time studying maps and talking with geologists. He convinced himself that there was oil—lots of it—hidden under the desolate plains. Not given to hesitation, Ricker leased the mineral rights to the state-owned ranch lands—674 square miles worth—in four counties west of San Angelo. Lease fees totaling more than $43,000 were due in thirty days. Ricker planned to sell a drilling deal to the major oil companies headquartered in Fort Worth. But the companies turned him down, convinced that West Texas had no oil.

The thirty days were almost up when Ricker ran into his old army buddy Frank Pickrell at the Fort Worth railroad station. Pickrell was no stranger to mineral ventures, having previously invested successfully in mining stocks. On the train Pickrell had made a new friend, El Paso merchant Hayman Krupp. Krupp, a Jewish dry-goods merchant and a millionaire, had sold supplies to both General Pershing and Pancho Villa during the recent border wars. Pickrell and Krupp had one thing in common: they were looking for a good investment. Ricker showed the pair his maps and leases, offering to sell them everything for $50,000. Pickrell and Krupp finally offered Ricker $2,500 for the leases. While it barely covered his expenses, Ricker took the money.

Pickrell headed west to check the leases, while Krupp went to New York to interest friends in a drilling venture. Failing at that, Krupp took out a personal loan from his bank to cover the $43,000 lease fees.

Pickrell and Krupp tried to sell stock in their new Texon Oil and Land Company. Painfully aware of the problems of having an oil company but no oil, they bought producing land in the Burkburnett field near Wichita Falls. They even drilled two successful wells there.

The firm hired self-taught geologist Hugh Tucker to study their land. Tucker outlined a promising area ten miles wide by thirty miles long and picked a drill site. The state allowed only eighteen months to start a well. Knowing that would not be enough time, Pickrell approached J. T. Robison of the General Land Office. Robison convinced the state legislature to extend the drilling time to five years.

Fund raising proceeded slowly. Texon had barely enough money to drill when Pickrell realized the five-year drilling deadline was at hand. He rushed to San Angelo, rounded up a rickety old water-well drilling machine, and convinced the conductor to hold the morning train while the machine was loaded aboard for the trip to the drill site.

Pickrell ignored Tucker's recommended drilling site and picked a spot next to the tracks. Legends have grown up about how the site was picked. One states the wagon carrying the rig broke down, causing Pickrell to drill at that spot. Another says the wagon got stuck in mud caused by a torrential downpour. Both stories are false. Pickrell deliberately chose his spot because it was close to the railroad tracks.

They did later drill on Tucker's recommended site. There they found nothing—a dry hole.

Drilling commenced on January 8, 1921, just before the

midnight deadline. Pickrell remembered he needed witnesses to verify the starting, or "spudding in," of the well. Spotting headlights on the horizon, Pickrell intercepted the car and convinced the men aboard to take him to San Angelo and to sign a notarized statement to that effect. Pickrell later discovered that the new law no longer required witnesses.

Many oil wells have been named for people, but this one was named for a saint. When worried Catholic investors from New York asked their priest for advice, he suggested the well be named for Saint Rita, Patron Saint of the Impossible. Saint Rita gained renown from caring for people in desperate circumstances. On her deathbed, in the middle of winter, she requested a rose from the garden. To everyone's surprise, there was indeed one red rose in the garden. Ever since, a red rose has been considered the symbol of Saint Rita. The group mailed Pickrell an envelope of red rose petals, which he sprinkled over the rig, christening it in Spanish "Santa Rita."

Pickrell hired R. S. McDonald, a rig builder from Big Spring, to build the derrick. As driller, he found Carl Cromwell, the "Big Swede." Cromwell moved his wife and baby daughter into tin-and-board shacks at the well site.

Funds were short. Drilling often had to be interrupted until more money could be raised for pipe, supplies, and salaries. Local cowboys often made up the drilling crew. Life wasn't easy at the well site. Mrs. Cromwell writes:

> Food was no small problem. Eggs, milk, butter, and fresh meats were not to be had. We had ice and fresh meats—come twice a week from San Angelo. . . . We ate a great many quail, which were plentiful, and so tame we fed them with the chickens in our yard.

Drilling continued through 1921 and 1922. On Friday, May 25, 1923, bubbles of gas started rising from the well. The crew boarded up the derrick and rushed to lease for themselves nearby land not already leased by Texon.

Preparing breakfast on Monday, they heard a roar and

Hugh Hardie Tucker. *From the Elizabeth (Tucker) Eaton Collection.*

Mr. and Mrs. Carl Cromwell, with their little daughter Carlene between them, at the Santa Rita No. 1 well. *From the Carlene Cromwell Peavy Collection.*

Levi Smith (left), President of Big Lake Oil Company, and Michael Late Benedum (right), Benedum-Trees Interests, at Santa Rita No. 1, 1924. *From the Abell-Hanger Foundation Collection.*

ran outside to see oil gushing over the derrick. It soon covered the shacks, greasewood, and even the chickens.

Interest in the well spread due to strong promotion by the San Angelo newspaper. Special trains left San Angelo, sometimes carrying over a thousand people, to watch the well flow.

Krupp and Pickrell started two more wells but didn't have enough money to finish them. No one else was interested in sharing Texon's fortunes. The major firms still felt that there was no real oil in West Texas. Desperate, Krupp and Pickrell approached the most famous wildcatter of the day, Mike Benedum. Benedum sent his right-hand man, Levi Smith, down from Pittsburgh to check out the prospects. Benedum paid off Texon's debts and agreed to drill eight more wells, in exchange for sixteen square miles of Texon's best leases and control of the new company, Big Lake Oil. Smith became president of the new firm.

Big Lake Oil seemed destined for failure. The next several wells held true to the belief that the Santa Rita # 1 was simply a small stroke of luck. Not until the last well planned, Santa Rita #9, roared in, did Smith know he had found an oil field. Other oilmen moved into the region, competing with Texon and Big Lake for well sites. Big Lake Oil built an elaborate camp for its employees, complete with school, swimming pool, and recreation hall. The town of Big Lake prospered. So did Best, a new and far wilder counterpart across the tracks. The oil field grew from nine derricks to dozens.

Santa Rita #1 wasn't the discovery well of the Permian Basin. That honor went in 1920 to the Underwriters Texas and Pacific #1. But the Texas and Pacific well, still producing today, received little publicity and made no stir in the oil world.

Royalty income from the vast state-owned ranch lands changed the University of Texas from a collection of surplus barracks into a modern school.

The foresight and work of these men, combined with a

strong streak of luck, created an industry in the Basin that changed tiny towns like Midland and Odessa into modern cities. For their efforts Ricker, Pickrell, Krupp, Cromwell, and Robison have all been inducted into the Petroleum Hall of Fame, located at the Petroleum Museum in Midland.

In honor of its role, part of the Santa Rita #1 is enshrined on the University of Texas campus. The Santa Rita #2, equipped with a replacement wooden derrick, is now located on the grounds of the museum.

Bibliography

Myres, Samuel D. *The Permian Basin: Petroleum Empire of the Southwest.* Vol. 1, *Era of Discovery.* El Paso: Permian Basin, 1973.

Orbeck, Betty. Interview with Mrs. Dee Locklin. McCamey, Texas, April 13, 1983. Taped and typed transcript, Archives Center, Permian Basin Petroleum Museum, Library and Hall of Fame, Midland, Texas.

Rundell, Walter, Jr. *Early Texas Oil: A Photographic History, 1866–1936.* College Station: Texas A&M University Press, 1977.

———. *Oil in West Texas and New Mexico: A Pictorial History of the Permian Basin.* College Station: Texas A&M University Press for the Permian Basin Petroleum Museum, 1982.

Schwettman, Martin W. *Santa Rita.* Austin: Texas State Historical Association, 1943.

All photographs reproduced courtesy of the Permian Basin Petroleum Museum, Library and Hall of Fame, Midland, Texas.

JIM HARRIS

The Rules of Cockfighting

No one knows why or when man first put fowl into a pit and let the game male do as he had done in the wilds for thousands of years: fight brother against brother until one cock ruled. No one knows why or when man first intervened and institutionalized part of the natural process that enabled the fittest to survive: the killing of all the competing roosters and the mating with all the hens. No one knows when game fowl were first taken from the jungles and bred in pens for their gameness.

What we do know is that the fighting of cocks was first the experience of the folk, that it became the passion of princes, generals, and kings, and that now it is again the pastime of the ordinary peoples of the earth. Historian Page Smith writes, "In much of present-day India, cockfighting has passed from the sport of princes and rajahs to the ordinary people of the country, who engage in it avidly, following formulas for diet and training several thousand years old. . . ."[1] But throughout the sport's history, cockers have always been a curious cross section of peoples. In his eighteenth-century diary, Englishman Samuel Pepys wrote, "To Shoe Lane to see a Cockfighting at a new pit there . . . but Lord! to see the strange variety of people, from Parliamentmen . . . to the poorest 'prentices, bakers, brewers, butchers, dairymen, and what not; and all these fellows one with another cursing and betting."[2]

Seventeen hundred years before Pepys wrote of attending a cockfight in London, the Romans came to the British islands, after having spread cockfighting throughout northern

Europe, and found the inhabitants raising chickens for amusement and sport.

Cockfighting came to the southwestern United States from two directions. From the south, the Spanish and Mexicans brought a long tradition of "slasher," or knife fights, the blades tied to the cock's feet resembling a curved, single-edged razor blade. Today knife fighting is done by Latin Americans, the Spanish, the Portuguese, and peoples in the southern Mediterranean countries, Asia, and the South Pacific. From the southeastern United States, cockers brought gaff fighting to the Southwest, the blades resembling a rapier with a sharpened point and a round body.

Biologists surmise that all domestic chickens come from the Red and Grey Jungle Fowl of India. The game chicken we know today is the chicken that most resembles in appearance and demeanor his fighting forefathers of the East. As in the wilds, he is combative with his fellow fowls, and this is what the cocker exploits when he puts two birds in a cockpit.

In the Southwest, owning, operating, or using a cockpit is legal in New Mexico and in Arizona, New Mexico being the only state with no laws covering the fighting of chickens in particular or cruelty to animals in general that might be applied to cockfighting. California has the strictest laws against cockfighting in the United States. There the sport flourishes. And in Texas, where cockfighting is also illegal, cockfights are held in clandestine and not-so-clandestine locations across the state.[3]

But whether they are fought illegally on the banks of Mill Creek outside Canton in East Texas, or legally at the elaborate Phoenix Game Club in Arizona, the birds are fought under some fairly uniform rules in several different types of fights passed down through the ages.

A *main* is a series of odd-numbered fights between two parties. The party with the most wins during the day or during a two-day period is declared the winner. In a main, cocks are matched according to designated weights.

A *tournament* is a method of fighting a predetermined

number of cocks at specified weights by a specific number of contestants. Several entrants are involved instead of just two.

Not fought often anymore, a *Welsh main* is a single elimination tournament in which a cock continues to fight in a series of battles until he loses, the winners advancing to the next round. The Welsh main usually begins with eight pairs of chickens, although these tournaments have begun with as many as sixteen pairs. Very few of even the best cocks today could take this sort of punishment since intensive inbreeding and line breeding have made competition very tough.

A variation of a Welsh main is called a *concourse,* in which not one but several different chickens are fought in each round. Again, this is not seen very much today.

Another fight not likely to be seen is the *battle royal,* in which many cocks are thrown into the pit and the fight proceeds until only two cocks remain which are to be fought by standard rules outlined below. In England the battles royal were often associated with what the English called *Shakebags,* matches in which the birds were leftover cocks not good enough to fight in regular competition. Today cockers call any birds over six pounds *Shakes*, and they are not fought in tournaments.

Still another type of fight is called a *hack,* an impromptu fight between two parties usually arranged at the pit, a fight fought, so to speak, on the spur of the moment. Hacks are fought before and following more organized forms of competition.

The most popular form of battle today is called the *derby,* in which many people are invited to enter cocks or stags (roosters before their first moult) which are secretly matched according to top and bottom specified weights. In a four-cock derby, for example, a cocker will have his four cocks secretly weighed, banded, and numbered. The birds will then be matched to others within two or three ounces. If there are thirty cockers entering the derby, 120 fights may follow, the winner being the one with the most victories. The actual number of fights will decrease considerably when cockers who have lost enough battles to know they will not win the derby drop out of battles with other losers. If the entry fee is $200, the winner will take home $6000 less a small percent for the house at some clubs. There is much betting on each fight. Usually the cocker or pitter will place a bet with his opponent before each fight.

Different sets of rules have governed the fights throughout the history of cockfighting in America, but since the 1950s the rules of Henry Wortham, "Modern Tournament and Derby Rules," have dominated.[4] (The editor of *The Gamecock* magazine, Faye Leverett, tells me that these rules were actually the brainstorm of a Dave Marburger, who let Henry Wortham, a famous cocker and referee, review and revise them before they were published.[5]) Most often, house rules are added, but they are not supposed to conflict with the Wortham rules which relate to gaff fighting.

Although in other centuries or other countries the pit was consistently circular, the cockpit in America can be circular, square, octagonal, or any shape as long as it is a minimum of sixteen feet across.

There are three sections to the Wortham rules. Section one relates matching the birds, the authority of the referee, the length of the heels, trimming, and banding. Cocks are matched, as stated earlier, at weights within two or three ounces of each other. The referee has final and irrevocable decision-making authority. Any length of heel that is round from socket to point is fair, although tradition and predetermined agreement may call for a short heel, 1¼ to 1½ inches, or a long heel, longer than 1½ inches. Trimming of the bird is allowed only with the tail, wing, and saddle feathers along with the feathers around the vent. All battle cocks and stags are "dubbed," have their combs and wattles trimmed to be less of a target for the opponent.

Section two of Wortham's rules deals with the actual fighting. Just before entering the pit, the referee weighs the cocks, checking the band numbers and examining the heels.

In the pit the handlers, called "pitters," are allowed to

"bill" the birds, allowing them to peck each other a few times while being held in the pitters' arms.

At the command of "get ready," the pitters place their cocks' feet facing each other. The cocks are eight feet apart at the start. On the command of "pit" the cocks are released.

Beak-to-beak pitting, called for under "Count" and "Time" provisions explained below, is performed with one hand. With the get-ready call, the pitter must have only one open hand under the bird, holding him in position. The center lines for beak-to-beak pitting are only twenty-two inches apart. After pitting on the eight-foot lines when the match begins or on center lines for beak-to-beak pitting, the pitter must stay at least six feet back from the cocks until the referee calls "handle," when each pitter must pick up his chicken.

The call to handle comes when one or both of the cocks is hung with a gaff. A pitter cannot touch the opposing bird except to remove the gaff hung in his own bird, and then he must grasp the opposing cock only below the knee and not lift him from the ground. Birds must be handled immediately when the referee so orders.

Between pittings after a handling, twenty seconds are allowed for Rest. At fifteen seconds into the Rest, the referee commands the pitters to get ready, followed in five seconds by the command to pit.

When the chickens are pitted, both will begin fighting most of the time. However, if one does not fight—and fighting can be the show of the least bit of aggression, including striking, chasing, or pecking—the opponent that is fighting is given "Count." Count is a way of determining a winner and ending the match. To initiate the Count, the fighting bird's pitter says, "Count me," and the referee counts to ten three times and he counts to twenty one time, taking a Rest of twenty seconds between each counting. If the other chicken does not fight in that length of time, the fighting bird is declared the winner. Again, Count is one of several ways to end the fight.

During Count, if the opponent *does* start fighting again,

the Count is broken, and a new Count begins when one bird refuses to fight and the opposing bird's pitter says, "Count me."

If the aggressive cock that has Count suddenly dies, the other chicken is declared a winner unless he is running away at the time. A runaway chicken is hated by all cockfighters, and a runaway can never be a winner.

When neither chicken is fighting, the referee has another way of ending the fight. Often they are just too weak to fight, or they just do not have the desire to fight anymore. When the referee decides neither chicken is fighting, he initiates "Time." This is a period in which he counts to twenty three different times, taking a Rest of twenty seconds between each counting. If neither cock fights during this period, the

fight is declared a draw. If both chickens are running away at
the end of the time period, each entrant loses a full fight;
there are two losers.

When one cock dies, the other cock is declared a winner
if he is not a runaway. If a cock dies during Rest, he must be
pitted dead a final time before a winner is declared. If both
cocks are mortally wounded and neither has Count, the referee may call a draw. If a cock leaves the pit, the remaining
cock may have Count until he is declared a winner; but if the
remaining cock is a runaway, Time is called.

A fight can last as long as the cocks can last. Usually,
after twenty minutes the battle is moved to a drag pit, which
may be only eight feet wide, where the contest is completed.
This moving of the fight is to keep up the pace of the derby, and

it may result in two or three battles occurring at the same time.

The final section of Wortham's rules concerns penalties. These are given for such violations as the use of unfair heels, not pitting when ordered, taking any action that will distract the birds, and the use of stimulants to revive the cocks. The referee has the authority to penalize a pitter with Count or to declare a winner when a pitter breaks a rule or commits a foul.

Again, rules may vary from place to place in the United States. At one time Sol P. McCall's "Rules of the Cock Pit" were most often used, especially in the South. And from time to time someone offers a new set of rules that have minor variations in them. But there is a remarkable similarity between the fighting of cocks at the present time and throughout the history of the sport.

In a 1937 WPA article in the archives of the Museum of New Mexico in Santa Fe, Reyes Martínez describes cockfighting in northern New Mexico before 1900 and relates a famous 1892 fight in Arroyo Hondo just north of Taos between two famous roosters, "El Giro" and "El Motas."[6] Although the pit was only a circle drawn in the dirt, the fight could have been conducted today in any small town in New Mexico or the Southwest. In one part of the narrative, Martínez describes the professional "amarradores," the "men who knew the art, for it truly was an art, of tying properly the knife to the rooster's leg. . . ."[7]

Halfway around the world in Bali villages, the tying of spurs is also a very special and honored job. Anthropologist Clifford Geertz writes of the tying of spurs, "This is a delicate job which only a proportion of men, a half-dozen or so in most villages, know how to do properly."[8]

Geertz related the importance of the cockfight to the communal life of the Bali villages, how it is an expression of male sexuality, how it reinforces the whole structure of the village, how it represents animality, how it is a release of violent impulses. But in the fights, he describes rules that are similar to Wortham's rules. The twenty-second division for Count, Time, and Rest occurs when a Balinese referee drops a coconut with a small hole in it into a pail of water. It takes the coconut twenty-one seconds to sink.

In the early part of this century, British sportsman Sir Herbert Atkinson wrote about cockfighting throughout English history and particularly about cockfighting in the eighteenth and nineteenth centuries when it was the rage in England. His book, *Cockfighting and Game Fowl,* describes battles beside English taverns and in the royal pits of kings—and in these descriptions the reader can find traditions of pitting and handling that are remarkably similar to those in the Southwest today.[9]

In the early 1960s, Haldeen Braddy published in a magazine, a newspaper, and a Texas Folklore Society publication a story of an exciting cockfight in Juárez between two famous cocks, "El Negro" and "El Blanco."[10] Although Braddy does not concentrate on the rules followed, the battle sounds like one that might be fought in Altus, Oklahoma, or Jackson, Tennessee.

Throughout the history of the game, cockers have been good sportsmen. Rarely in the pits today will one see a discourteous pitter; hardly ever will one see arguments with the referee as in football or basketball or baseball. Though there are questions among cockers about rules, they accept these rules and the referee's judgment as authority and as part of the traditional comradery among a fraternity of game fowl lovers that has its roots in folkways established long before there were such things as masons or hockey teams. In a 1949 book called *The Art of Cockfighting,* famous American cocker Arch Ruport writes:

> The cocker's fraternity is one of the greatest in the world. It has no officers or by-laws, and its members pay no dues. Yet there are rules, and they are honored and respected by all true and honest cockers. The sportsmanship of the members of the fraternity is seldom equaled and never surpassed in any other branch of sport.[11]

One final note in conclusion from Page Smith in his inquiry into the rise and fall of *Gallus Domesticus:*

> . . . we must certainly be aware by now of the fact that history contains no form of behavior relating to humans and their animal companions which is higher in symbolic meanings, or which penetrates more profoundly into the inner recesses of the masculine physic life than the cockfight, almost everywhere forbidden and almost everywhere practiced. [12]

Notes

1. Page Smith and Charles Daniel, *The Chicken Book* (Boston: Little, Brown and Company, 1975), p. 115.
2. Samuel Pepys, *The Diary of Samuel Pepys,* ed. John Warrington (New York: Dutton, 1953), p. 470.
3. Giles Tippette, "The Birds of Death," *Texas Monthly,* November 1978, pp. 163–65, 271–77; Dick Reavis, "Texas Monthly Reporter," *Texas Monthly,* September 1977, pp. 78–81.
4. *The Gamecock* magazine holds copyright to the Wortham rules and publishes regular articles on rules and interpretations. Copy machines have made possible many issues of the rules, and they can be found in other publications, including Arch Ruport's *The Art of Cockfighting* (New York: Devin-Adair Company, 1949), p. 149.
5. Letter from Faye Leverett, January 4, 1985.
6. Reyes Martínez, "Cock Fights," WPA writing in the archives of the Museum of New Mexico, Santa Fe, May 25, 1937.
7. Martínez, "Cock Fights," p. 1.
8. Clifford Geertz, "Deep Play: Notes on the Balinese Cockfight," *Daedalus* 101 (Winter 1972), p. 8.
9. Herbert Atkinson, *Cockfighting and Game Fowl* (1938; reprint, Surry: Saiga Publishing Company, Limited, 1981).
10. Haldeen Braddy, "Feathered Duelists," in Mody C. Boatright, Wilson M. Hudson, and Allen Maxwell, eds., *Singers and Storytellers,* PTFS XXX (Dallas: Southern Methodist University Press,

1961), pp. 98–106; Braddy, "Feathered Duelists," *Pass Word,* Spring 1962, pp. 70–74; and Braddy "Cocks Aren't Chicken in Border Sport," *The Southwesterner,* January 1964.

11. Ruport, *Art of Cockfighting,* p. 3.

12. Smith and Daniel, *Chicken Book,* p. 124.

All photographs reproduced by permission of F. E. Abernethy.

John Chadbourne Irwin standing by the abandoned forge from Camp Cooper, around 1935. The holes in the forge were made by buffalo hunters sighting in their rifles in preparation for hunting along the Clear Fork of the Brazos River in the 1880s. *Courtesy of the Irwin Collection, Hardin-Simmons University Photographic Archive.*

LAWRENCE CLAYTON

The Family Saga
An Interpretive Analysis

ALTHOUGH bonafide sagas stem from Medieval times in Scandinavian countries, the form has evolved into what C. Hugh Holman in *A Handbook to Literature* calls "a form lying between authentic history and intentional fiction."[1] One modern type of saga consists of stories that develop in families and serve as the oral, traditional lore of that family. These narratives, which resemble the early sagas in scope, tend to be even more episodic, less chronologically arranged, and less "heroic" in content than examples of the early Scandinavian form. Folklorist Mody C. Boatright considers family saga the "lore that tends to cluster around families, or often the patriarchs or matriarchs of families, which is preserved and modified by oral transmission, and which is believed to be true. Lore that is handed down *as* folklore is excluded." Boatright continues by saying that family sagas are "not concerned with a type of tale, but with clusters of types, not with a motif, but with many motifs."[2]

The stories of my concern differ somewhat from those Boatright discusses because they are more personal and less spectacular than his, and they provide more of a sense of community within the family. These family narratives are universal only in the sense that they represent a framework for particular events related to the life of a given family. Some of the stories involve members of other families in the action, either as antagonists, as co-protagonists, or as observers.

The cycle of family saga is a fragile organism developed

in a sympathetic environment and is susceptible to upheaval and decline when the circumstance that created the saga changes, especially when the context around the pivotal figure alters in any way to break the dynamic chain of creativity and recreation through telling of the stories. For example, my initial awareness of these narratives developed years ago from the stories my grandfather told of his exploits as a young man in South and East Texas, which are now, unfortunately, so dimmed by time and by not being told that they are lost. He told and retold these stories as we worked together when he was teaching me of life and of farm and ranch work in East Texas in a tutor/tyro relationship. He was one of the most important heroes of my early years, and his philosophy and outlook as revealed in these stories have shaped my life. When my family moved back to town, the link between my grandfather and me altered, and the tales told freely in the work environment were stymied in the more polite circumstances in which we only occasionally found ourselves after that. When he died some years later, I realized how fatal to the cycle is the loss of the pivotal figure, for that absence destroys the environment necessary for the development and continuation of these stories. Usually the family gatherings so vital to the cycle either cease or alter in structure to avoid the tales and thereby to avert the poignancy of loss felt by other members of the family when the central figure is recalled through the stories.

My interest in this form of folklore was rekindled by the tales I heard my father-in-law tell and retell after 1958, when I married into the West Texas pioneer Irwin family and began to spend weekends and holiday periods at the Irwin Ranch near long-abandoned Fort Griffin, a post–Civil War military post located on the Clear Fork of the Brazos River between Albany and Throckmorton in Northwest Texas. These stories dealing with the western frontier sparked my interest, as had those my grandfather told me. The setting for the Irwin stories is much like that found earlier in my grandfather's stories, a rural one, this time loaded with the romanticized elements of the West Texas ranch country. This region is still dimly peopled by figures from the past like then-Colonel Robert E. Lee, commander of the nearby pre–Civil War military outpost named Camp Cooper; early-day cattlemen like the Hittsons, Gentrys, Reynoldses, and Matthewses; outlaws like John Wesley Hardin, John Selman, and John Larn; and even living legends like Watt Matthews, son of Sallie Reynolds Matthews, whose family saga is told in *Interwoven: A Pioneer Chronicle.*[3]

The patriarch of this cycle of stories is J. C. Irwin, Jr., a mild-mannered, reserved, but vivacious modern-day frontiersman. Mr. Irwin was born in 1902 within a mile of where he lived during most of the years I knew him. A third-generation Texan, he grew up along the Clear Fork of the Brazos River on the Irwin Ranch where he helped farm and tend the cattle. He worked in the West Texas oil fields as a tool dresser, roustabout, and pumper until he retired in the early 1960s and moved a house onto his part of the family ranch. This modest structure provided a home for Mr. Irwin and his wife, LeIta. Although not large, the Irwin ranch, which has been in the family for over one hundred years, encompasses some four hundred acres of rolling, mesquite-dotted range land which has provided the opportunity for the extended Irwin family to work cattle, hunt, fish, and spend sizeable amounts of time together in a relaxed environment with little stricture on the language or content of the fairly cohesive set of stories that became the Irwins' oral storehouse. The twenty miles of space between the ranch and Albany, the nearest town, provided a healthy degree of isolation from outside influences during our visits there.

I came to realize just how crucial a productive context— an outdoor work/recreational one—is to the development of this oral tradition as I have known it. Given this kind of context, it seems that the development of the cycle is a natural manifestation of a narrative tendency in people and will occur unless negative circumstances are present. For example, the tendency of some religious groups to treat jokes and stories with disdain is detrimental to the cycle's development. The reluctance seems related to the religious injunctions against "idle tongues." Also the desire of that generation just out of the rural experience to sever ties with that part of their past and join in the urban existence seems another negative factor. There are likely others as well.

The cycle of relating the stories seems predictable. I found that as new members have joined the family, usually through the marriage of one of the family members, such as my own daughter and later a niece, the same spate of stories would be retold in no particular order over a period of several gatherings. Some of these were told by my father-in-law; others were related by those of us who had heard the tales and repeated them from memory. New stories have been added in the form of narratives of adventures involving me, my two brothers-in-law, and other members of the family. Upon occasion, when only those individuals familiar with the stories were present, an allusion by a phrase or two from one of the stories would elicit the desired effect associated with the complete tale. The purpose might be to evoke laughter, emphasize a point, or note a contrast in a situation or behavior. I found as well that many of the tales were told and retold either at the dining table as we sat after meals or on the front porch, a favorite spot for relaxing on a summer evening, usually with a chorus of coyotes in the background. Significantly, no radio or television set is found in either location to interfere with the flow of conversation. I began writing these stories down some years ago and have continued to add to the overall collection since that time.

The specific incidents in the cycle of stories in families vary, of course, from family to family, but the general makeup of the saga has similarity in the kinds of material included. The stories are typically of a few distinct kinds. One concerns coping with hard times growing up and is related to stories dealing with the Great Depression, a common motif for those who lived through that dismal period. Another category involves jokes and pranks, which may or may not be work re-

J. C. Irwin, Jr., his wife LeIta, and their first child, Dale, around 1925. *Courtesy of the Irwin Collection, Hardin-Simmons University Photographic Archive.*

lated. A third kind recounts remarkable occurrences or tales of adventure. A fourth variety includes stories related to historical events or personages.[4] Some examples will illustrate.

The story which actually got me started on this project involved Mr. Irwin's childhood and is a "hard times" tale. Although similar to depression stories, this one does not involve the Great Depression at all. It seems that during his childhood he faced a series of depressions. I will relate the story as nearly as possible in Mr. Irwin's words:

"Yes, I've had plenty of hard times in my day. I remember once when I was a kid, my brother Firl planted a crop of watermelons in that old sand field west of the Robison place, and the folks planted some cotton too. This never was farming country anyway, but it rained some that spring for a change, and we were hopeful. Grasshoppers were real bad, too, though—those old big jumbos, some were three or four inches long, and they did like cotton stalks and leaves, nearly ate us out of house and home. Dad put me and my brothers in the field with wooden paddles, almost like flat baseball bats, walking the rows and killing hoppers. It wasn't much sport, after a time, I can tell you. Human insecticide I guess we were, but there wasn't much other kind. We also took a turning plow and cut a furrow all around the field with the straight side toward the crop. The hoppers would try to climb that— they can't fly, you know—and they would fall into that trench. We'd mixed wheat bran with strychnine and syrup and put that in the trench. They'd eat that poison and die by the thousands, but it didn't kill nearly all of 'em. But we just couldn't give up and let the hoppers have the cotton. We killed grasshoppers all through late June, but we looked forward to the Fourth of July. We usually had a get-together with the neighbor families at the Red Top School, which Dad built in 1907 for us kids to go to school in. I figured we could let them ole hoppers rest for one day. I hoped maybe the hot sand would kill 'em, but I noticed they seemed to thrive in it. It didn't appear to hurt their feet like it did my bare ones, 'cept I do recall [he chuckled] how we used to kid about some of those hoppers carrying other hoppers across that hot sand to save their feet. We knew about hopper reproduction, I guess; it was just a kind of a kid joke.

"About the first of July, Firl carried off and sold a wagon load of his big, sweet melons. Me and my brother Stanley sneaked one down to the draw and ate it that day; we didn't tell little Jimmy. He never could keep a secret. The Fourth dawned kinda mixed. By late morning, a cloud was coming up, and I knew there'd be no party at the schoolhouse that day. By noon the sky in the northwest was as green as winter wheat, and I felt a puff of cold wind when I was out at the barn puttin' stuff up from the wettin' we knew was comin'. Before two o'clock it hit, the wildest hail storm you ever saw. Come right out of the northwest, broke out all of the windows on the north and west sides of the house. Covered the ground! Hailstones as big as golf balls piled up two or three feet on the sides of the house! Lasted about twenty minutes, I guess. When we went out, it was awful. Trees were stripped; everything was beaten down. It even killed some rabbits and bruised up the cattle some. My brother grabbed a saddle horse out of the barn and rushed over to check his melons. It was as useless as everything else we did to try to get ahead in those days. Those melons looked like somebody had shot all of 'em with a Winchester 30-30. Cotton stalks were stripped bare of leaves, just stalks standing there. I knew it was all lost. We all went over and ate all of the melon we could hold, knowing that was all we'd get out of it. When we got back home we noticed those hailstones just melting there. Ice in July! Now that was a treat too good to pass up! We gathered up some while Maw mixed some sugar and milk and eggs together. We put that in an old crank freezer, filled those hailstones in around it, put some stock salt on it, and kept cranking till we had a freezer of cream. That was one of the few times I had ice cream in the summer 'til years later. Never have quite got all I wanted, even yet.

"Well, that wasn't the worst of it. You know, the rain and all that melted hail fed that cotton, and it come out green as could be, grew a second growth like crazy. We were foolish enough to get excited about pickin' cotton that fall. The strippin' had set it back considerable, and that fall, kinda late for cotton, it began to make squares. Just before those squares would have opened to make cotton, frost hit it. It wasn't particularly early; the cotton was just late because of the back-set caused by the pounding of the hail. All the cotton we picked that fall was just 'bout enough for Maw to make three quilts. It struck me then—we'd worked hard all summer; we killed grasshoppers and hoed that cotton and those melons. All we got to show for all that hard work was all the melon we could eat one day and a freezer of ice cream the same day. The two together gave me the worst bellyache I nearly ever had."

Life was undoubtedly hard, but those who survived responded with humor, often seen in the form of jokes and pranks. These are easily illustrated from the Irwins' storehouse of tales. The following prank served to straighten out a problem for the group and had a useful, not a destructive, purpose. It occurred when Mr. Irwin was still a child in school.

"Well, I learned to throw rocks chunkin' at the outhouse the girls had out behind the school. Us boys just went to the creek. I got where I could hit that pipe coming up out of that outhouse every time I throwed. My throwin' nearly got me in trouble one time, though. Louis Overton—we called him Sandy—and I were older than most of the other kids by this time, and we felt an obligation to help out around the school. Robert Tuton—Grace's brother—had trouble gettin' along at Fort Griffin School and was moved up to Red Top with us—an exchange student, I guess you'd call him now. His mother, who had a nickname for everybody, called him Dobbin. 'Be beautiful, Dobbin,' she'd say to him. It didn't work much, though. He was bad to pick on the little kids, bullied them a lot. Well, one morning Sandy and I were out playing catch before school when Robert began to pick on some of the little kids. I knew he needed a fire built under him; Sandy and I got the idea at the same time. He moved over to put Robert in line between us and waved at me to throw the ball. I lined up on Robert and hit him right in the back of the head, just below the rounding spot on his skull. Whump! He went down and was out like a light. The girls screamed and ran, and the teacher came chargin' out. Robert came around after a little and began to cry and say he was bad hurt. The teacher decided he wasn't, but she had us all in and asked around and decided that it was all an accident. She told me and Sandy to go back to playing, but she made Robert stay in. He slowed down some after that but not much."

In this case, the story has a moral—bullies deserve to get abused—and illustrates the ability to inflict punishment with impunity for a right or just cause.

Another incident related to the school experience involves getting the best of the teacher who, as misfortune decreed, lived in the Irwin house, near which the small school had been erected. She treated the situation with some disdain, which prompted Mr. Irwin to pull the prank on her that he did. He recalls the incident this way:

"Her name was Margaret Robinson, and she was from somewhere up in North Texas. Her sister taught up at Throckmorton at that time. She stayed in the east bedroom of the old ranch house on the river, the one that burned. There was a piano in her room, and she could play a little. We had a telephone by then—it was about 1912 or so—and she'd call up her sister in Throckmorton and talk to her. She didn't take to country living too much and didn't make any bones about it. It was Halloween. Donald McKechin was due to come visit, and she'd been sittin' around on the porch, waitin'. But she got bored and called up her sister in Throckmorton and said, it being Halloween night and all, she didn't know how to act out in the sticks. When she lived in town, they'd always go out and trick-or-treat on Halloween night.

"Well, I listened to her runnin' down where we lived and decided I'd scare her a little bit. I've always been a little devilish, I guess. Well, Dad had an old bearskin rug that was lined real nice. We used it for a lap robe or cover in a buggy. It was 'bout dark, so I got that old bear robe and a set of buffalo horns that'd been made into a hat rack. By this time she was off the phone and was back playing that piano. I got to the door and propped it open just a little bit. Then I scratched on the screen. She quit playing and listened. I was real still. Then I scratched on the screen a little bit more. She got up to see what was going on. Well, I had that robe all around me and those horns tied on my head, and I came growlin' and groanin', jumped in that door and hollered 'Whee Hoo!' When she saw me she lit a shuck screamin' that the ol' devil who was out there was out there with his horns on. She ran the length of the house, through that bedroom, the room next to it, just a flyin'. My brother Ennis was sittin' in the third room, which was the kitchen, in a chair by the cook-stove. She was so scared she left a string of water all through those three rooms and still had enough left to wet Ennis down good when she jumped into his lap. Maw was there and laughed so hard she could hardly catch her breath, but it was tough at home and at school for me the next few days after that. I don't think that teacher ever forgave me. She finally married Joe Overton and lived around here till she died."

Mr. Irwin had many exciting adventures, but one which has come up regularly in the conversation involves an experience he had some years after I came into the family. The Irwins at that time had Lucky, a small, part-bulldog canine that served as a watchdog. He often treed varmints in the post oak trees that surround the Irwin house. Mr. Irwin loves to relate this story:

"One evening as I was fixin' to go to bed, I heard Lucky barking and recognized the bark that he had treed something. I knew that if we were to get any sleep that night, I just as well go out and take care of whatever Lucky had up that tree. Taking my flashlight and my .22, I walked up nearly to the road where I could tell Lucky had something in one of the oak trees. When I got to him, I shined my light into the tree and saw a pair of eyes gleam back. I figured it was a coon, so I aimed just below the eyes and fired. Something dropped from the tree, and Lucky grabbed it and ran into the broom weeds before I could tell what it was. When I walked under the tree to see if I could figure out what had fallen, I felt something warm dripping on my head. I raised one hand to my head and came away with blood on my head and shoulders. I backed up under the tree, shined the light into the branches again, and saw eyes gleam back. I shot again and a half-grown bobcat came crashing down.

"As near as I can figure out, the bobcat must have grabbed a rabbit; lots of 'em live in the grass and weeds around the house; it's safer for 'em there. Lucky saw 'im get it and took in after 'im. The bobcat, rabbit in its mouth, got up the tree to get away from the dog. My first shot wounded the bobcat and made him drop the rabbit, which Lucky grabbed and carried into the weeds. The second shot, of course, brought the bobcat down."

That story is guaranteed to send the grandchildren to bed early any time it is told. The effect can be elicited by referring to Mr. Irwin as a man who shoots rabbits out of trees. The horror element—the narrow escape from being clawed by a dying bobcat—is strong in the tale.

The Irwin family has strong historical ties in the region. Mr. Irwin's grandfather came to the Clear Fork area from Fort Chadbourne to the southwest as the first sergeant of a dragoon company stationed at Camp Cooper and later, after he had left military service to begin ranching, provided beef to the soldiers at Camp Cooper under a contract signed by Robert E. Lee, by then the Commander of the Department of Texas. These events happened in the late 1850s. In addition, the family "forted up" at Fort Davis in Stephens County during the latter stages of the Civil War, a period documented ably by Sam Newcomb's diary appended to Sallie Reynolds Matthews's *Interwoven*. Elmer Kelton used that material at the beginning of his novel *Stand Proud*.[5] This body of lore, however, has been in oral tradition so long that it has lost much of the detail necessary to provide a narrative framework and any characterization at all. None of us alive, even Mr. Irwin, knew the grandfather, who was killed by a thief in Fort Sumner, New

Mexico, in 1867 as he returned from a trail drive to Kansas.[6] Therefore, the personality around which the tale would revolve is too dimmed by time to be an anchor point for the narrative. Tristram Coffin makes a point in regard to folk ballads that seems relevant here: the longer a ballad is in oral tradition, the less narrative and the more lyric it becomes. The same seems true of these tales which, lacking the mnemonic devices of rhythm and rhyme, have less support for recall than do the ballads and lose any narrative structure or cohesiveness. Massive distortion of facts is also likely in that part of the narrative that remains.[7]

One history-related story still told about Mr. Irwin's father, whom he does remember well, involves an incident in which John Larn, notorious cattle rustler and former sheriff of the town of Fort Griffin located in the flat below the military post on the Clear Fork of the Brazos River, nearly killed Mr. Irwin's father, John Chadbourne Irwin. The younger Irwin usually tells the story this way:

"My dad knew John Larn was rustling cattle because Larn sold beef to the army nearly every day, but the size of his herd didn't drop off any. Dad lost three big ol' steers he used as oxen and went to the Larn place to check on them. Larn's slaughterhouse stood on a bluff on the river, and a deep hole of water was just below that bluff. Dad walked out to the edge of the bluff and looked into the river and he could see lots of beef hides weighted down with rocks in that hole of water. He wondered how many brands were on those hides, but he never found out. Larn walked up about that time and said, 'Mr. Irwin, do you see anything?' Dad glanced over and saw that Larn was patting the pistol he always wore. Dad said, 'No, John, I don't see a thing,' and left. But later Dad was part of the posse that arrested Larn and carried him to Albany, where some masked men broke in and killed him. I've heard that they were members of Larn's wife's family." The historical authenticity of this story is born out in Carl Coke Rister's *Fort Griffin on the Texas Frontier*,[8] but the account is somewhat embellished by legend.

These stories stabilized or gave focus to countless family conversation sessions that otherwise included a plethora of current gossip, information about the affairs of past and present friends and acquaintances, and stories related to the families established by the Irwin children in their own communities. The gatherings were richly rewarding. As in all things temporal, however, these times could not last forever. Regrettably, I have rediscovered how fragile is the existence of the context producing these stories. After I had pretty well completed collecting the principal tales, the eighty-three-year-old Mr. Irwin had a stroke and lay three days and nights before he was found in the ranch house, where, after his wife's death in 1973, he had lived alone. He now lives in my home, paralyzed on his left side, his mind clear and his speech still audible. But the happy context for telling the stories is gone. The tension generated by disagreement concerning his care among the three sisters—one of them is my wife—has fragmented this family unit probably forever. The family circle is broken and with it the cycle of stories. It is fortunate that the research was completed before this development in the life of this family, for these stories would otherwise be headed toward extinction since the framework for rehearsing and renewing them is gone.

The value of these stories to the formal study of folklore is yet to be fully understood, but the tendency to tell tales is as old as mankind. In this age of fascination with prepared stories in books and films, this may be the most natural form of oral narrative still being practiced.

Notes

1. C. Hugh Holman, A *Handbook to Literature*, 3rd ed. (Indianapolis: Odyssey Press, 1972), p. 471.
2. Mody C. Boatright, "The Family Saga as a Form of Folklore," in

Ernest B. Speck, ed., *Mody Boatright, Folklorist* (Austin: University of Texas Press, 1973), p. 124.

3. Sallie Reynolds Matthews, *Interwoven: A Pioneer Chronicle* (1936; reprint, College Station: Texas A&M University Press, 1982).

4. See Jan Harold Brunvand, *The Study of American Folklore*, 2nd ed. (New York: W. W. Norton Co., 1978), p. 114. He uses these roughly equivalent categories: misfortune stories, personal experience stories, favorite anecdotes about eccentric relatives, nicknames and expressions of a family group, and the like.

5. Elmer Kelton, *Stand Proud* (New York: Doubleday, 1984).

6. See Lawrence Clayton, "A Gun Slinger Confesses: The Story of John G. Irwin," *Old West Magazine,* Fall 1982, pp. 17–19.

7. Tristram P. Coffin, "Mary Hamilton and the Anglo-American Ballad as an Art Form," in MacEdward Leach and Tristram P. Coffin, eds., *The Critics and the Ballad* (Carbondale: Southern Illinois University Press, 1961), p. 249.

8. Carl Coke Rister, *Fort Griffin on the Texas Frontier* (Norman: University of Oklahoma Press, 1956), p. 158.

PAUL PATTERSON

Showdown at Sunup

Within the span of four years I inflicted upon you two nightmares in the form of two escaped night horses, Buster and Pullwater. Each beast, as you recall, left me afoot and stranded. And, as you recall, being forced to walk, to a cowboy, is a fate worse than the frontier female's fate worse than death. I also led you to believe that the gravity of my situation ranked a notch above that of Mustang Gray (he of the song) and second only to that of the unhorsed cowboy who was forced to walk from Yellow House Canyon to Fort Concho, a distance of two hundred miles.

I hereby and forthwith "abhor myself and repent in dust and ashes."[1] Now it sorrows me to say so, but the Pullwater catastrophe, for example, is as sounding brass compared to that of my ten-year-old brother, Fush, some fifteen years earlier and not fifteen miles distant, as the buzzard flies, from the second "Night Horse Nightmare."

On the lad's skinny shoulders rested the fate of not only himself but that of Papa, Babe (our beloved work mare), and twenty-five or thirty head of cattle, not to mention the Bob Harlan gray, which no Patterson can mention without seeing red, he being the beast that set them afoot five miles from water and twenty miles from home.

To snare the Harlan gray Papa had contrived a Rube Goldberg–type contraption, the description of which defies description. This he had, time after time, sprung on or rather *at* the critter, each miss marking one step closer to total wipeout of the Patterson cattle empire, the end of the noted XE Bar brand.

Thus far it had not occurred to Papa to give Fush a go at the gray. Or perhaps it *had* occurred to Papa but to have done so would have been an open admission that his (Papa's) reflexes were shot. Or perhaps it was because he was painfully aware of the lad's propensity for maneuvering molehills into mountains.

In any case, Destiny, or something, dusts off the deck and deals Fush in. So now: the scene, setting, and stage whereupon is about to unfold the final action-packed act of this spectacular showdown between a sixty-pound boy and a thousand-pound horse with no quarter asked—or given.

TIME: Around sunup of a July morning, 1916.

SETTING: Patterson camp in Granger Canyon, enclosed in an unwatered, four-section pasture in the extreme west end of Crockett County, Texas. In the foreground sits a wagon. In the wagon sit four cypress wood barrels (all empty except one, which is almost). In the back end of this wagon sits a chuck box, its lid down to form a cooking-eating-dishwashing table. On the table sits a tin dishpan in which sit the breakfast dishes. On and about the dying embers of a campfire sits here a coffee pot, there a frying pan, yonder a skillet, over there a bucket of dishwater on to heat and so on.

Off to one side sits the "contraption" consisting of a tall cedar post slanting out over a half-barrel watering trough. Suspended from this post is the spread-open noose of a lariat rope, sustained so by a mish-mash mess of wires groping out in all directions like the tentacles of an octopus. The great, gray tentacle reaching and clutching a hind wheel hub of the wagon would be the other end of the lariat. Some thirty feet away from the contraption, at the end of one tentacle—the trigger tentacle—sits Fush.

In the background can be heard the bawling of thirsty stock, a few of which can be seen, crowding closer to the water trough. Foremost amongst the herd lurks old Bob Harlan Gray himself, emboldened by thirst and by the fact that Papa is nowhere to be seen. Now the critter inches a step closer. He is surmising, and rightfully so, that he has, at last, caught the old man with his pants down, for Papa, at that very moment, sits back in the greasewoods answering nature's morning call. What old Gray does not know is that in situations such as this, Papa has authorized Fush to spring the trap.

Moreover and *most important*, the critter does not know he is facing a far more formidable foe in Fush. Not only are the kid's reflexes faster by far than his father's but his head is fuller of guile. That is to say, when it comes to trickery this kid has been there before. Fact of the matter is, ol' Gray is a gone goslin' and doesn't know it. Fact of the matter is, his horse face shows quite the opposite, an expression of total confidence intermingled with utter contempt. If ever a beast is on the verge of throwing his head back and letting go with a hearty horse laugh old Gray is the horse.

Part of the Patterson family near Roscoe, Texas, in November 1918. From left: John, Gwen, Papa (John D.), Fush, and Paul (the author). *Courtesy of the author.*

But first to quench the worst of thirsts. He steps boldly forward, souses his nose under and drinks to the full extent of his oxygen supply. Now then. A violent exhalation of air will add emphasis to a contemplated, contemptuous snort. He throws his head up, then back (the height of hauteur), his upper lip curled preparatory to same when ZZZZZZZTTT-TTT, a snake-like something seizes him by the windpipe, throttling him completely.

This does not preclude, however, a violent explosion of air, but a blast not to be interpreted as a snort of triumph, being as how it is emitted from the other end. One explosion calls for another—and another and another and another in rapid succession. Rapid enough to be considered semi-simultaneous (if I may coin a phrase here) and of a magnitude to register three-point-three on the Richter Scale.

Explosion number two is old Gray himself exploding into action, hitting the end of the rope, which act triggers a chain reaction of explosions: the chuck box exploding in a shower of exploding cans—soda, baking powders, sugar, horseshoe nails, coffee, axle grease, and so on—not to mention a shower of tin plates, cups, pans, exploding from the dishpan.

Only the old wagon, being of stern Rock Island stock, stands its ground. Better yet, it stands off a stern challenge from the half-mustang Bob Harlan gray. This is not to say it remains totally unmoved. Its rear end is jerked violently around, not to mention almost off. Now it stands shivering, shuddering, and shaking like a wet dog, scarce able to hold its tongue.

The final explosion—two to be exact—so synchronized to sound as one, comes from Papa and Fush in a last laugh. What the Bob Harlan gray does not know and does not need to know is that not *all* of this horse laugh is at the horse. Part of it is from relief. However, most of the laughter was to come later—at family reunions, funerals, weddings, etc.—speculating as to what must have been happening to Papa all this time. Some even made so bold as to suggest that had the old gray been aware of what was passing with Papa, he (the horse) would have felt vindicated to a considerable degree.

In conclusion, I deem it only fair to confess that the expression, "Wherefore I abhor myself and repent in dust and ashes," is not original with me. But rest assured the source is duly documented and footnoted as per instructions.

Note

1. Job 46:2.

Marguerite and Harmon Lowman—fifty years battling the devil and ignorance. *Courtesy of the author.*

AL LOWMAN

Elephant Ears in the Churchyard

Iꜰ Staples had been quite the Paradise that Daddy described, then a preacher should have felt as lonely and useless as a Maytag repairman. But Staples supported two churches—Baptist and Methodist. With admirable evenhandedness, Colonel John D. Staples had given each denomination an acre of ground on which to build.

He knew these churches were needed. To illustrate the point, his grandson Dudley Sherrill of Baytown tells about the time (around 1908) that the Whitten youngsters—Frank, Robert, and Willie—caught a buzzard in one of their traps. They stuffed it in a tow sack and hauled it home. At dark thirty the following evening they took the buzzard from the barrel where it had been stored, attached a cowbell and a ten-foot length of tin wire between its legs. To the trail end of the wire they tied a small bundle of kerosene-soaked rags.

After lighting the rags they turned the buzzard loose to ascend the soft night air to the accompaniment of a loudly clattering cowbell. It circled once or twice for orientation, then headed west, which meant that it flew practically the length of town. Supper had just ended in most of the homes, and now the occupants rushed out onto their porches to ascertain the cause of the commotion. All they could see was a trail of fire across the sky. Some thought it was Pentecost all over again. Since this story was told to me as the gospel truth, perhaps it bears repeating in New Testament cadence:

And suddenly there came a sound from heaven as of a rushing mighty cowbell, and it filled all the houses where they were sitting. They began to speak with excited tongues, as the Spirit gave them utterance.

And there were dwelling at Staples devout men and women out of every state under the Confederacy. Now when this was noised abroad the multitude came running. They were all amazed and were in doubt, saying one to another, What meaneth this? Others mocking said, These folks are full of new wine.

But down at the post office the next morning a savant lifted up his voice, and said unto them, Ye men of Staples, and all ye that dwell at Staples, be this known unto you, and hearken to my words: The Whitten boys done it!

Doubtless the buzzard clawed the wire loose from its foot within moments of its return to the roost. But I asked ninety-two-year-old Bill Whitten if he'd thought about animal cruelty when tying the bell between the vulture's legs. "Oh I reckon it come off after a time," he replied, "but I never seen a buzzard that had to sneak up on his lunch anyhow. Besides, that bell kept them other buzzards skeered off, so he had the whole meal to hisself. Why that was probably the fattest buzzard in five counties, and he had the pick of the roost to boot!" Obviously the boys had done it a favor.

Well, there was a lot of opportunity in Staples for moral uplift all right; less so for charity, if Great-Grandpa Scott were to be believed. In combing old church records three years ago, Ted and I discovered a 1917 conference report that the old man had submitted as conference secretary. Among the questions to be answered, one stood out: "What is done for the relief of the poor?" There followed a neatly inscribed reply: "We have no poor." In Staples the poor were not neglected; they simply were not seen. They were invisible even to themselves. The community was and is what James J. Kilpatrick has said of Richmond, Virginia, "a hotbed of social rest."

Religion, however, was taken seriously in Staples. When its young people left, they had had the seal of their upbringing firmly impressed into the wax of their personalities. Uncle Harmon, Daddy's oldest brother, was a college professor and later administrator. Aunt Marguerite was the daughter of a preacher, the Rev. W. L. Hightower, who once used a crank handle to demolish the radiator of a Model T that wouldn't start. (I always felt that preachers should be people that other mortals could identify with.) Aunt Marguerite was gray-haired, keen-eyed, gracious, crisply efficient, indomitable, and unwavering. She and Uncle Harmon made a helluva team.

Frequently Uncle Harmon was invited to fill church pulpits throughout East Texas. Standing five feet ten and weighing about two fifty, fill them he did. His weight problem was most conspicuous when the families camped each summer at Grandpapa's old farm. The high point of each day was inner-tubing down the river. Uncle Harmon's girth was such that he fit snugly into a tube that had been stripped from a ten-twenty truck tire. He would enter that tube with all the suspense of an overweight ballerina trying to stuff forty pounds of leftovers into a junior-size tutu.

One day in the late 1930s Uncle Harmon was driving between Lufkin and Nacogdoches. In the car with him was a presiding elder of the Methodist Church. As they passed through the Redland community Uncle Harmon mentioned that he had spoken on Layman's Day some five or six years earlier "at that Methodist Church yonder." He nodded toward a structure on the right side of the road.

"Harmon, that's the Baptist Church. The Methodist Church is up here on the left. It used to be hidden in the pine trees until they cut 'em all down."

Uncle Harmon confidently reasserted himself. "Well, I spoke back there to a Methodist congregation. They had a wonderful turnout, too. Couldn't seat 'em all."

He remembered the occasion vividly. As he had pulled into town that Sunday morning, he had it fixed in his mind that the Redland Methodist Church stood adjacent to the school ground. Sure enough there was a church, right where it should be. Running late, he wheeled into the driveway, parked, exited from his car, bounded up the stairs through the double doors and down the aisle to the altar rail, where he presented himself to a silver-maned, bespectacled gentleman who bore the mark of authority.

"I'm Harmon Lowman from Nacogdoches. I was asked to give your Layman's Day address."

The man in charge gave a polite but vaguely puzzled response. "And who did you say you are?"

Uncle Harmon merely assumed a communications failure and repeated, "Harmon Lowman. I'm your district lay leader."

"I see," replied his dignified host. There was a twinkle in his eye that escaped Uncle Harmon's notice. After a moment's hesitation he said, "Let me go tell some folks you're here," at which point he disappeared briefly. Again Uncle Harmon detected nothing amiss. On his return the silver-domed gentleman in glasses escorted Uncle Harmon to one of the vacant chairs behind the pulpit. Looking over the crowd they saw a sanctuary that was nearly filled. Then suddenly a great mob of people appeared in the door. The remaining pews were quickly filled and people were left standing in the aisles. Uncle Harmon glowed with quiet satisfaction at the very remembrance of the event. Quickly his reverie was jarred by the voice of the presiding elder seated next to him in the car.

"Harmon, that was the Baptist Church; the Methodist Church is right over there." The P.E. motioned with his hand as they passed.

Uncle Harmon knew that presiding elders could be as thickheaded as any department chairman, so he slowed to a virtual stop and U-turned in the road. They backtracked to the scene of his triumph. As they pulled into the driveway he saw, for the first time, the modest lettering over the doorway: FIRST BAPTIST CHURCH.

In time, he evolved an explanation. When the silver-haired, bespectacled Baptist preacher realized that Uncle Harmon was out-of-pocket, he didn't want to embarrass him, so he sent word up the road to the Methodists telling them, "We got your speaker down here, why don't y'all come join us?"

No wonder there had been standing room only in the church that morning. It amazed Uncle Harmon that no one—not one—had ever let it slip that he had been in the wrong place at the right time. Perhaps it had been a demonstration of Christian charity. Freshly minted Ph.D.'s sometimes need a lot of that. Certainly the Baptist preacher saw an opportunity to save his own sermon for a rainy day.

There was no denying that Uncle Harmon's appearance had been a great popular success. He was not unflattered when many in the audience subsequently expressed a fervent wish that he might serve them full time. The reasons for such obsequiousness are not difficult to uncover. To begin with, the Baptists had never heard a fifteen-minute sermon before and could not believe that such a thing existed. Second, both congregations were thunderstruck when Uncle Harmon declined an offering to pay his honorarium and travel expense.

For his sons and nephews he later had this advice: "If any of you boys ever get to be a lay leader, remember your most important job is to show up in the right church!"

No sooner had Uncle Harmon's ego recovered from this trauma than came another. About 1943 he was invited to speak one Sunday morning at the Methodist Church in Centerville. He and Aunt Marguerite were chauffeured by their son Bill. Uncle Harmon had been college president at Huntsville for only a short time, a war was on, and the press of many responsibilities had prevented him from preparing a text, but he felt it would be safe to extemporize.

Immediately prior to his introduction from the pulpit, the preacher called upon the congregation to sing "Hymn 259—What a Friend We Have in Jesus." The congregation responded faithfully and fervently. With Aunt Marguerite and Bill seated in the congregation before him, Uncle Harmon was introduced. He expressed the usual felicities and then launched into his theme, which dwelt on the need to bring more than one's physical presence into the house of the Lord. Now here was a surefire topic—a safe one, too. Still, despite unimaginable odds against it, he managed to shoot himself in the foot. Let me confess right now that I'm going to give you the Revised Standard Version of this story, because that's all I ever heard.

He began by saying that "worship isn't solely the minister's responsibility. Each of us as individuals must concentrate our hearts and minds and souls on the meaning of the words we hear and the words we utter. It is not enough," he vowed, "to give an occasional nod in the minister's direction as he reads from the scriptures; it is not enough to mouth the words of the responsive reading without awareness of its message; it is not enough to sing idly along while our thoughts wander out the window. To praise the Lord in music adds a sublime dimension to the worship experience. There's a sermon in every song."

By this time Uncle Harmon was warming to his subject. Picking up the hymnal which lay at his elbow, he continued: "This grand old book contains countless expressions of God's love and mercy for his children. You need only open it at random to see what I mean." At this point Uncle Harmon proceeded to follow his own suggestion. Waving the open book before him, he declared, "Here, now, is a perfect example. Hymn 259—What a Friend We Have in Jesus. How long has it been since that inspired music has been heard within the walls of this church?"

The color was draining from Aunt Marguerite's face. Her reactions under stress were not always predictable. On this occasion she reached over and pinched Bill on the leg—to get his attention—and then hissed between clenched teeth, "Doesn't the damn fool realize we just sang that?" Bill's infuriating response was to lean back and enjoy the debacle.

By this time Uncle Harmon was clearly on a roll. "How long has it been since you concentrated on its wonderful message of comfort, assurance, and salvation? How long has it been since you brought these words to life and sang them from the heart? How long?" As soon as the service was ended, Aunt Marguerite told him.

I have come to believe that every family—regardless of denomination, and even heathen—has at least one member somewhere in its ranks who is without question "The Finest Methodist Lady in Texas." In our family Aunt Marguerite was a prime candidate. About 1960 she and Uncle Harmon were traveling in the Midwest with their three grandsons and a nephew who was the age of the grandsons. They ranged from six to nine. It was Sunday morning and Aunt Marguerite had already announced that they would be stopping for church services along the route. The boys were dressed in T-shirts and blue jeans and looked scruffy as usual. The plan was to stop beforehand at a service station and clean them off a bit.

By and by, Aunt Marguerite spotted a suitable station and turned in. As the car was being serviced, she asked the attendant how to find the First Methodist Church. Seeing the Texas license plates, the man replied: "Lady, church will be starting in about five minutes. You crossed into another time zone about twenty miles back."

Instantly Aunt Marguerite herded Uncle Harmon and the boys back into the car. Without waiting to listen carefully to all of the directions, she gave the man five dollars, told him to keep the change, put the car in gear, and dug out. The attendant barely had time to retrieve the pump nozzle and replace the gas cap.

The oldest grandson, who told me this story—and who is not sufficiently imaginative to recite anything but the truth—says he was looking out the rear window as the car raced away and wondering how he was going to make it through church without going to the bathroom. The last thing he saw, he says, was a cursing attendant being stung with flying gravel just before being enveloped in a cloud of choking dust.

Twenty-five years later the boys doubt that they ever made it to the First Methodist Church that day. Aunt Marguerite simply pulled into the first Methodist Church she saw. Early arrivals had taken the back pews, so they had to parade down to the front, looking like leftovers from *The Grapes of Wrath*.

As misfortune would have it, the congregation had just concluded a six-week study of the books of John and were to be tested that very morning. Everybody got a copy of the exam and a pencil with which to complete it. Names and addresses were specifically called for. Aunt Marguerite set about with a flourish to answer the questions. Uncle Harmon took a stab at it and then decided, as the better part of valor, to submit his paper anonymously.

The boys fidgeted and stole glances at each other's blank forms. Finally, so as not to turn in a perfectly clean sheet, one of them lettered neatly at the bottom of his quiz: "I have never been in this state before in my life." The only thing the boys got out of this exercise in futility was a subsequent lecture from their granddad that they should never try to cheat on a test—especially in church.

Two weeks after their return home, Aunt Marguerite received a letter from the pastor congratulating her for having maxed the exam—adding gratuitously that no member of his regular congregation had even come close.

The search for perfection never ends. Neither does the evolution of family folklore. One morning in the early Seventies I was commuting from my home in Stringtown to the office in San Antonio. As I passed New Braunfels, a dude wearing a narrow-brim hat got behind me in a battered GMC pickup and started tailgating. This continued all the way to Selma. When I sped up, so did he. When I slowed to a crawl, he followed suit. When I resumed speed, he was right behind me. I had just about decided that I had a mental case on my hands when suddenly he swung to the left, accelerated, and started to pass. As he pulled ahead, I saw the sticker on his rear bumper: "I have decided to follow Jesus."

I can't figure it out. Was it a case of mistaken identity? Or one of those wonderful spiritual conversions on the road . . . to San Antonio?

A true story.

LORA B. GARRISON

Hog Drovers
The Why and How of Hog Drives

The stories I tell are true stories about the early settlers of the Frio Canyon Hill Country, which lies on the southern edge of the Edwards Plateau in the region of the Balcones Escarpment. The heart of this area is Leakey, Texas (in Real County), in the upper end of the Frio Canyon. Leakey is forty miles north of Uvalde, and Uvalde is eighty-three miles west of San Antonio, Texas.

The wild hogs in this story were simply domestic hogs that had been turned loose to fatten on masts. Some of the remnants of these hogs have crossbred with the imported European hog called the Russian Boar, and the present, resulting breed is truly fierce and sought by sport hunters.

I have been collecting oral history in this area for six or seven years, and the following information and conversations are the result.

The annual hog drive was one of the most unusual things that ever took place out in the Frio Canyon. In the late 1800s the ranchers used to have these tremendous hog drives. You have heard about the cattle drives; well, these were hog drives. Can you imagine taking a thousand or two thousand hogs and driving them to market, just like they drove cattle? That's what they did.

My grandfather, Alex Auld (who had migrated from Scotland), was one of the men in the community who started the hog drives. The others were William Puttum Whittum Holmes (migrated from England), Fred Large, Drew Large,

Dave Huffmon, and my grandmother's brothers Pete and Bud Lowrance. They all gathered their meat hogs in the fall of the year. There were hogs by the hundreds out there on the ranches. The ranchers would round them up and get them ready to go to market.

These folks had a lot of land, and they didn't have fences dividing the ranches to keep things separated. It was all open country, so they had let their hogs go wild, and the hogs had scattered. The hogs roamed the woods searching for nuts and sweet shin oak acorns, which were real good to fatten hogs on. But that was before the boll weevil.

The drovers had real good hog dogs. Fred Large had a bunch of old hounds. When one of those hogs would break out of the bunch, those dogs would run, first one way, then the other, until they would tie into the hog and chew hell out of him. When he got back into the bunch he was mighty glad to stay there. He wasn't going to get away from the rest of them hogs.

It took six weeks to two months to gather all those hogs. The ranchers would hold the hogs until they got ready to sell them. They had good pens made of stacked rails up there at my grandfather's place, and everybody would bring their hogs to this one place. It was called Maverick Camp. The small pastures, probably a thousand acres, had good seven-wire fences. This is where they would hold the hogs after the hogs were gathered. There were a lot of shin oak acorns in there for them to feed on.

There was one thing the ranchers would always do, if they found some real gentle old sows, you know. You would think this would be pretty good. But, no, that wasn't the kind they wanted, because those gentle sows, they wouldn't protect their pigs. The ranchers would take any sows that seemed to be gentle and spay them, and cut off their tails. A gentle sow would go off and leave her pigs. So the ranchers got rid of the gentle ones. In about two years the spayed ones would be big meat hogs. These hogs would get fat and would be ready to bring into town and sell. The real mean ol' wild sows were the ones the ranchers wanted to keep out on the ranch, because these would protect their pigs and wouldn't let the varmints get them.

The ranchers would mark all the male hogs and cut most. When a particularly mean ol' boar hog wouldn't stay in the bunch, he would be roped around the snout behind the tusks, and then tied up, watching out he didn't thrash around and cut somebody with his sharp tusks. Then his eyes would be sewn shut so he would stay with the other hogs. These hogs would be three or four years old and some of them had long tusks. They would cut hell out of those dogs if they could catch them. Those dogs had better stay out of their way if they wanted to live. It took a mean hog to catch a good dog.

Dave Huffmon's son Jake recalled seeing Alex Auld catch a hog.

> Mr. Auld used to get down and get an ol' hog to run at him, and he would catch it by the ear and reach over and get it by the hind leg and flip it over and tie it up. Daddy told him he better use a rope; he was going to let one of those hogs get him some day. It wasn't more than a week and one of those ol' boars caught him on the wrist and ripped it open. He was a tough ol' bugger, Mr. Auld was. He sewed it up with a spaying needle he carried all the time. The needle fit in a grooved piece of board and had a waxed thread wrapped around it.
>
> Old Man Holmes brought his hogs up across country from the Holmes Ranch, and he stopped there at what's Bob Ramsey's place now, to give them salt. When he got out there to Maverick Camp he wanted to turn the hogs out and water them. Course, that was the wrong thing to do, to turn out a bunch of wild hogs with those that was wilder. When the deed was done the hogs all stampeded. Ran all over the country.

Jake told me that he was on that particular hog drive.

Alex Auld and Fred Large during a hog roundup at the Auld Ranch, about 1898. *Courtesy of the author.*

Uncle Pete Lowrance was running the outfit. That was after ol' man Auld died. Pete let 'em turn them fresh hogs out with the tired dogs, and Daddy tried his best to keep him from doing it but he wouldn't listen. He turned them out anyway. God, they jist stampeded like a bunch of blackbirds. Lost about half or a third of 'em. There was only about four hundred left. Dogs was tired and couldn't hold 'em. Daddy told him not to turn them hogs out 'cause they'd stampede and we'd lose the whole thing. But Holmes wanted to turn them out and water 'em in a dirt tank. We had to gather for about three days after that 'fore we could leave Maverick.

My Uncle Dan, Alex Auld's son, told me:

Ol' Fred Large and ol' man Holmes, they was out and the dogs caught one of ol' man Holmes' hogs. Fred tied him down. He tied the legs across each other, all four of them, and put him up in the

A hog drive to Sabinal, about 1905. From left: Drew Large, Holmes Ferguson, Luke Large, Walter Large, Fred Large, Cal Bell, and Jeff Thompson. *Courtesy of the author.*

saddle and put the legs over the saddle horn and then got up behind him. That's the way you carry a hog in. Ol' Fred Large got that one, and he came in there and he turned around to ol' man Holmes and he said, "Mr. Holmes, do you want to water him before we put him in the pen?"

When they got them hogs all back in there and got ready to leave, Mrs. Auld said, "Pete, Uncle Bud is takin' these hogs from here on." My daddy got in there with a black snake whip, and God he sure mixed those hogs of Holmes' up with the other hogs before they left with 'em.

Jake's wife Maude remembered:

Mrs. Auld rode an ol' white mule with a sidesaddle on them drives, with a long black skirt, Aunt Susie did. She went with 'em. That was after Uncle Alec got killed by the horse. She'd ride that ol' white mule and go help drive those hogs.

Jake reminded Maude:

> Mrs. Auld didn't go on to Kerrville. She'd go up to
> Maverick Camp. She helped gather them hogs
> back there though, them three days. She went with
> Drew Large out there gatherin' them hogs. Drew
> had a good dog and a good horse. Them dogs would
> bay a bunch of hogs, and he'd cut that horse loose
> as fast as he could run, and time he'd pull up there
> at them dogs, Mrs. Auld would be right behind
> him, there on that ol' white mule. Said he never
> did get far away from her, everywhere he would go
> she would be right there. She would get there jist as
> quick as he could on his fine horse. Oh, she was a
> bearcat on a horse. I don't guess anything ever
> came by that she couldn't ride. Long as she could
> get that ol' sidesaddle on it, she could ride it.

Uncle Dan told me:

> We would probably throw in a thousand hogs in
> one drive from the ranch to Kerrville. The way we
> done it, we always had a few ol' pet hogs around the
> ranch house, and they would learn to eat corn and
> were gentle too. We would put a wagon in front of
> them with a load of corn. Not just shelled corn; it
> was corn on the cob, ol' dry corn on the cob, and
> somebody would have to sit in the back end of that
> wagon and shuck and shell this corn off, and the
> gentle hogs (they were called Judas hogs, you can
> figure out why), they would eat this corn, and the
> wild ones would follow them. We would drive them
> about ten miles a day, and we had pens where we
> would pen those hogs at night. They would bring
> those Judas hogs back home and use them again,
> because they would lead the other hogs to slaughter.
>   That was a sight to see, a thousand or two
> thousand hogs in one bunch. There would be ten

or fifteen drovers ride along the sides with their dogs. That was after the railroad was built into Kerrville. It would take about five days to make a drive. They done that for quite a few years.

Jake explained:

We had a couple of feed wagons to haul feed in for the hogs and one empty to haul hogs that got down and couldn't travel. Those hogs them days, weren't too stout in their hind legs. They was weak and they would get down like a bear. You would have to haul them hogs, maybe the second day. The third day they would all go. Wouldn't have to haul none of them. They jist wasn't used to traveling. They was fat, fat and too heavy on them ham strings; they would get down. That's the reason you had to have the extra wagon.

Daddy had to put a muzzle on a bunch of hogs; they were awful mean. Those cut boars will fight anything. I thought they was going to cut the legs right off my ol' burro. I'd be scared to death.

We would start out from Maverick Camp; that was Mr. Auld's place. First day out we stopped at South Fork Ranch. Next night we stopped at ol' Will Alexander's, down there around ol' Gid Marsh's the third night or the fourth night. We would try to eat dinner there at what we called the Glass Lake. One time there, after dinner, some of the boys were sleeping under the wagon when I decided to play a trick on them. Gathering up the trace chains, I began to beat on the wagon and holler, "Woah! Woah!" Those fellers hit that wagon about three times before they could get out from under there.

One night while camped at South Fork—it was plenty hot—we asked Jeff Thompson, one of the drovers, to pray for cool weather. He was a sort of a preacher feller. Well, he prayed and about two o'clock in the morning the darndest norther blew in there and about froze us to death. The next day several of them ol' boys put Jeff over the wagon tongue and whopped him with a pair of leggins. He took it in pretty good humor. This was a custom of cowboys, you know, when someone displeased them. They would give him a whoppin' with the leggins. As we went on into Kerrville, down below ol' man Secrest's mucky bluff on the Guadalupe, the seep springs had icicles hanging all over them that evening. Ol' Jeff jist overdid the thing a bit.

One campground was along about Ingram at the Schreiner hog pen, there on the right where all the improvements are now. We kept them there the last night before we brought them on into Kerrville to the railroad.

There is an interesting thing about those drives. Back in those days everybody trusted each other. They didn't have to count every hog and prove how many hogs they had. When someone brought their hogs in they would say, "I brought 800 hogs," or "I brought 500 hogs," or "I brought 1,000 hogs." When they got their hogs to market and sold them, they divided the money up that way.

Uncle Dan told me:

We got three, four, or five cents a pound for those hogs. We was mighty lucky. We made more money out of hogs than we did anything. That hog business. There's nothing like that, of course, today. It couldn't be. You couldn't drive them on the road if you had them.

The boll weevil is what finally killed off the hog business, by killing off the acorns. The boll weevil would puncture the sweet acorns and lay an egg in there; it would hatch and the worm would eat the inside out of the acorn. No more acorns, no more fat hogs to drive to market.

MRS. JOHN Q. ANDERSON

A Key of Golden
Brief Encounters Remembered

THE dusk and twilight of that June evening were as comfortable as summer provides in the beautiful piney woods hill country of North Louisiana. The weather is sometimes too humid, sometimes too dry, sometimes unbearably hot, but the evening is always fanned with soft breezes to welcome the night.

My mother thought she heard a baby's cry, but my brother, then about nine years old, believed it was a tomcat caterwauling. He, as confident as the Biblical David, took his slingshot and fired six pebbles against the garage wall. The noise continued.

A neighbor, wondering "who in the world's blankety-blank baby" Mother was keeping, called. He offered to come help restore peace and quiet to the weary neighbors. My mother, who thought it was his baby crying, had been about to offer to help that child; so she said, "I guess it is just tomcats!"

"Tomcats!" Mr. Clay Skinner exclaimed. "I am going to see a tomcat that cries like that!"

He struck out and came to our garage. There, wrapped too warmly for the climate, lay a baby almost on the auto track. Mr. Skinner hurried back to his house and called my mother and the coroner. The three of them went together to lift up the infant and to bring it into our house.

I was puzzled that the medical doctor had left the baby there, but that was a puzzling year to me. I had just learned the previous Christmas that Santa Claus was not real, for my gift, a handsome wicker doll buggy, was left under the tree with a price tag still on it. The foundling was laid in my doll buggy, which was large enough for a three-year-old child and had a moveable canopy and brakes. A neighbor dashed my elation by telling me that the baby was not ours, and the coroner sent me out of the room while he discovered the sex of the baby. When I was permitted to return, the baby was sound asleep where my dolls had lain before. It was the first time I had ever been near such a young human being.

Dr. J. J. Bennett, the coroner, was at the scene of an accident when he was called. He was followed to our house by many of the townspeople who turned out in great numbers to fires and accidents and to watch the trains go by.

I was designated mother's helper to politely turn the curious people away from our door the next day, after the very extensive press notices attracted crowds to town. I recall being pushed and shoved and jostled by people who filled the rooms and the hallway. I roved about amid the knees of the strangers who did not notice me or pay attention to my place of authority.

Mr. and Mrs. C. E. Covington had been sitting on their front porch across the street the afternoon of the abandonment. They reported having seen a woman wearing a long cape and walking south on our street. They had seen her turn at our corner. Shortly after the police had their description, the officers picked up a woman with a cape and a suitcase at the Red Onion Cafe. They found baby garments in the suitcase. The woman, whose husband was in prison, had had a previous illegitimate baby in his absence. She had been working as a housekeeper for a redheaded railroad engineer in Texas when she "got with this child," who was born in the Shreveport Charity Hospital.

When the engineer was brought to the parish courthouse, my parents sent me on an errand so that I would not be in the way. I happened to be leaving them at the door just as the officers escorted the man into the building. He acknowledged parentage and signed a release for the court to give my parents full custody of the child for care and for placement for adoption. My father enjoyed walking with "Little Buddy" in his arms. I was entranced by the white diapers flapping on the clotheslines and by the wonder of it all.

It was not long until a couple came with empty suitcases, and my parents released Buddy to them. My parents cried together, for they would have kept him had his history not been too well known in the area for him to have had a fine life.

I remember nearly everything about having that baby in our house and about what went on during that time. I recall that five hundred people came into our house that first day before the police could provide protection. I discovered that there was a lot of information for me to learn before I would be ready to start growing up to be an adult.

There were a number of unexpected brief contacts with people whom I have remembered all of my life for the reason that they added something to my understanding of things, though I knew very little about the individuals at that time or since.

A Redbone man and his dark Cajun bride came to the North Louisiana hills to live, and my Christian father knew about them. I overheard him telling my mother to be kind, thoughtful, and generous to them because their status put them at a disadvantage. The black Negro did not like the "high yellow," and neither of them regarded the Redbone well. The little wife, by grace of the Catholic Church, had been given dispensation to be married, though the Redbone had more than a tenth Negro blood. They would be away from the festivities of their previous environment. She had a new baby.

The chance of seeing a second baby at a very early age was of much interest to me. One morning, in the midst of a twelve-lady bridge club luncheon that my mother was having, the cook, who had permitted me to sit still in her kitchen, looked out and exclaimed that the woman and her baby and an old lady were "heading for our house." I knew they were the Redbones, and I begged the cook to ask my mother to let me have them eat with me. My mother sent word that I could play hostess if I would be of no trouble to the servants, if I would set the table on the back porch, and if I would clean up afterward. She told the cook what I could use of the party refreshments and gave me permission to make a shrimp and apple salad.

The little mother had walked two miles to come to show off her little baby. The older woman was her grandmother. She had come "to be with her," as adults said then in connection with giving birth. They were pleased to eat with me. The grandmother sang me a wistful, sad song when I asked about music in their world. The words were "The day is over / I walk across the fields / The sun is set / I am returning home / Tomorrow will be the same."

She told me about the sadness of life and did not speak of joy. All the while the infant slept and the mother smiled. I felt what all must come to know: that bright spots of life are mostly stored in the heart out of tribulations and hardships that are the larger part of life. I remember these people, and I am thankful for their gift of insight to me.

When I edited the Minden, Louisiana, newspapers, each workday morning I arose very early to be at my office by 7:30 A.M. One block from my rooming house (now the Webster Parish Library) a tall, erect gentleman, Dr. Luther Longino, came down the steps to his porch and joined me. He was ninety-four years old and he still kept his office open, being much in demand to certify birth dates of "his babies" for government jobs and other records. He had delivered most of the native population. His unpretentious office was reached by the steepest flight of stairs I have ever seen. It was tended by Tom, a 103-year-old Negro who had been born in slavery and given to the infant Luther as his companion.

"You young people move too fast," Dr. Longino told me. "It is no wonder you die with heart attacks." He said that one must set a reasonably steady pace and keep it. I would match his gait, and I have kept it and his wise admonition to this date.

I think of this fine man as an example of how professions were *callings* and how once-upon-a-time professional people exemplified good character, ethical conduct, and dedication to their service to others.

At almost eight o'clock one morning I raced out to start my newsbeat and noticed a small child huddled in the alley. I stopped and asked her what the trouble was and if I could help her. The cold-gripped child turned a tear-streaked, frostbitten face upward and sobbed, "I am cold." When I wrapped her in my arms and shared my jacket, she revealed that, because her parents lived less than two miles from the school, she and her two brothers had to walk to school. A bus was supplied for those living greater distances. That cold day, without adequate clothing and no gloves, this shivering child was hurting physically. I took her to my office, called the school officials and her mother, and raced out to buy her some mittens. Her name was Loretta and for the rest of the school year, she and her two brothers stopped by each afternoon to show me their papers and report cards and to eat ice cream with me often.

Like one's own children, these temporary children of mine swiftly grew away, but they filled a very lonely life with pleasant moments when they were around.

A couple came into my newspaper office one day from the Red Cross building across the street. They told me that the director would not help them. They were fairly ordinary looking, and I was immediately sympathetic. It turned out that their son was a prisoner of war and they had been given a form that was approved for contacting their son. It was not long before I sensed that they could not read or write and that they had not told the person at Red Cross that. Without alluding to that matter, I suggested that I type the letter in order to send more messages. I asked a great number of questions about his friends, his kin, his brothers and sisters, and I finally got a short paragraph in my own words. I asked how they would like to sign the letter, meaning "with love" or some other affectionate phrase, and I could see that they retreated, lest they admit they could not write. Then, I realized that they were more interested in whether his allotment would come to them, for they mentioned that they feared he had changed it.

I understood that they belonged to a too-large group of people who are incapable of expressing or are unaware of how to express love, and who go through life without knowing any higher emotion. I knew then that this young man would know that his parents had not written the letter. I added a short note telling him I had made the letter from what they had told me, and I thanked him for his service to our country.

I have thought about those parents and the soldier son many times. The bounty of my life with loving and educated parents calls that young soldier to mind whenever I tend to indulge in self-pity, whenever I meet people who do not take advantage of the opportunities for betterment that are all around, and whenever I hear a person claiming a right to things that must come from within and through his or her own efforts.

The two soldiers were heroes with Purple Hearts and other citations. The mother of one of them had called for me to interview them for my newspapers. When I arrived, she ushered me into their bedroom where they had apparently eaten their breakfast served in bed and were still lolling. They greeted me almost as if they thought they were "in fun city on leave." I feigned to ignore their bare chests. I told them that I would give them five minutes of my time to get dressed and to come into the living room if they wished to give the interview that their mother had requested. "Heroes come into my office nearly every day of the week," I said. "They always have their clothes on!" Within four minutes, they sheepishly presented themselves. There are more ways than one to tell real heroes.

The police department called for me to come over to the jail to see what a woman detainee might need. She had been picked up in a hotel room with seven men who had dice-fixing and gambling equipment in their car. She was bruised from head to toe. She was a much battered woman.

I introduced myself as the editor of the local newspapers

and told her I had come to see if she needed anything. She whined that she "wanted to call her mother" from whose presence she had been missing for eight weeks. She painted a verbal picture of a concerned and dutiful daughter, but I told the police chief that she more likely wanted to call "the boss." She did not seem to be concerned about the bruises, and she had no interest in sanitation. I always remember this sleazy creature when I run into situations in which it is hard to know what to do when the "lioness wears sheep's clothes and moves with guile."

Taking a pause in my Fat Stock Show census taking, I was about to get on the Ferris wheel when a Negro maid asked if I "would let the babies ride" with me. The two babies were three and five years old, and the younger one had a lighted, hand-rolled Bull Durham cigarette in his hand. When I exclaimed, "Look what this child has picked up!" the nursemaid told me that they were "Mr. Blank's boys" and that he let them smoke and drink liquor because "they might not live to grow up or to have any fun." We took the ride, and I was the only one of the three who viewed the fun through a child's eyes.

I later learned that the children, known as "Mr. Blank's bastards," became all-round petty thieves and "hellers on horseback at drinking parties" with their father and his sharecropper woman. Mr. Blank's legitimate son had drowned in the bayou at age eighteen a few years before, and the mother had suffered a breakdown and permanent mental troubles. After Mr. Blank's heart attack, he built a house a rifleshot's distance from his home for his pore-white housekeeper. These boys had resulted.

When some of the ladies of the Baptist Church tried to help this woman to an ethical way of life, she told them that she had everything she wanted. She had a big automobile and expensive clothing; she had regular beauty parlor appointments and all of the *True Story* and *True Confession* magazines in print.

As our society has gone more and more to the acceptance of vegetative reproduction of their kind, recalling this foursome gives another example of what is not meant by parenthood.

It was a busy day, the time news was scarce, and I dashed into the drugstore to get a snack. All of the serving stalls were occupied, and I overheard an elderly woman with a young boy talking to the waitress. I realized that she did not have enough money to buy what they had come to get. I told them that I was in a great hurry and needed to eat a quick lunch. I said that I would be pleased for them to be my guests for whatever they were ordering if I could sit with them. My offer was accepted. The grandmother told me where they lived in the country and a great deal about their life. They were very poor, but they were not without the wealth of a good faith in God and pleasure in small things. Her eyes sparkled and laughter punctuated her speech. The nine-year-old boy, eating his first ice cream cone, impressed me. I savored his enjoyment. I suspected that not many people ever get to share a moment like that one.

I was riding horseback alongside Bayou Macon as the day was nearing dusk. I spied a tiny child, not quite as tall as the crop, in the midst of an uncut hayfield. She had scraggly yellow hair and a pixie face. I pulled up the horse and asked where her parents were. She waved her hand to the east. I told her I would wait there until she "ran along" to her parents, and she trotted off toward where no one and no houses were evident. Then the horizon swallowed her. I rode on toward town. I never found anyone who knew who she might be. I would not be sure that she was real had I not taken a snapshot of her there alone in that field.

I remember that child's blending into the soft shadows of twilight. I remember my riding homeward into the sunset in that North Louisiana Delta land where the sky falls on the earth like a dark feather comfort with the coming of night. I remember that unknown child and the era when both she and I could be safe alone on the edge of a wilderness.

Note

The year the little baby was abandoned was probably 1927. The event was reported nationally by radio and newspaper reports, and visitors and letters came from all over the United States. However, the local newspaper files and those for the leading newspapers in this area are not available for the 1920s period. Some have been destroyed by fire. The Redbone family came the same year. All of the other incidents took place in the years between 1939 and 1946 in North Louisiana.

ERNEST B. SPECK

Summer Revival

T HE summer ritual of revival meetings in rural Texas varied from community to community, although certain elements were universal. I want to tell of the pattern in my home community of Lone Grove in central Texas during the Great Depression.

At Lone Grove there were usually three meetings each summer: Baptist, Church of Christ, and Methodist. In a sense of fairness, there was a rotation in the order of the meetings. That accounts for the fact that old lady Cook spent each year in a different church. She joined each sect during its meeting, and at the end of the summer she was Church of Christ, Methodist, or Baptist—depending on the denomination that held the concluding revival—until the next summer's meetings. She was no less adamant about her current faith each year than about the others, and she rested secure from September to June that she had chosen the right path to glory.

For years, meetings had been held in brush arbors which shaded the faithful and others from the treacherous Texas sun. At Lone Grove in about 1930 the community built what we called a tabernacle, pronounced "tabernickle." In some places these buildings were called "permanent arbors." The tabernickle at Lone Grove was built of materials salvaged from the old one-room schoolhouse. New heavy cedar posts for supports had to be acquired, but the roof beams were made of old two-by-fours (which actually measured two inches by four inches), boards from the walls were used for decking, and shingles were carefully removed and used again. Cousin Charlie McCall said that it was more work to pull the old building down with its seasoned lumber and square nails, than it was to build the new structure.

The tabernickle was a true folk building since no professional builder was involved. It followed the general pattern of the brush arbor, but it had several advantages. First, the roof would turn rainwater with no more than a minor leak here and there. Second, there were no spots where the sun came through, as was sometimes the case with the brush arbors. The only time sun was a problem was during services after "dinner" on Sunday afternoon, when those sitting on the western side caught the afternoon sun. But those who did sit in the sun, did so quite stoically; it was seemingly a measure of their piety that they suffered without complaint as they listened to the Word.

Another advantage was that there was much less likelihood of spiders descending from the brush covering the arbor. Finally, of course, was the fact that fresh brush did not have to be gathered for each summer's meetings. A disadvantage was that there were some creatures who sought shelter under the roof for nests: dirt daubers, yellow jackets, wasps, and wrens. A community project was to go to the tabernickle before meetings started and clean out these intruders, along with evidence of birds' nests.

The tabernickle was about thirty-five feet square and would seat about two hundred people. The benches (to call them *pews* would be an excursion into fantasy) were from the two (later three) local churches, plus some built solely for tabernickle use. At the front of the tabernickle was a low platform some eight by fifteen feet on which there was a lecternlike pulpit from one of the churches, and unless the meeting was being held by the Church of Christ, a piano, usually canted a bit, across one of the back corners of the platform. Most preachers needed the fifteen feet or so of platform to pace across while exhorting their listeners.

On each side of the platform were four or five benches. One side was for the choir, an unrehearsed group of people known to be good singers. An indication of the strength of feeling between the sects was that members of one church would attend the services of other churches, but my dad for example, reputed to be the best male singer in the community, would attend the services, but he would not sit in the choir at a Baptist or Methodist service. The benches on the other side of the platform formed the "amen corner."

Lighting for night services was done by a direct-current system powered by a gasoline generator, the lighting source for the local country store and the storekeeper's house. It was hauled up for each meeting, and the store reverted to kerosene lamps for a time. Thus night services were punctuated by the beat of the gasoline motor. The forty-watt unfrosted globes attracted flying creatures of all kinds, giving evening services an added dimension. Preachers learned not to stand directly under a light lest circling moths enter their mouths as they took a breath.

In addition to the benches and the lighting, two other types of equipment were in evidence. Hymnals were provided by the local church holding the meeting and others close by. For example, if there was a Baptist meeting at Lone Grove, there would be no services at Bluffton, some ten miles to the east on the gravel state highway, so the Bluffton hymnals would be available. The hymnals were paperbacked, and the Church of Christ hymnals had shaped notes, although many of the same songs appeared in both books. When a good crowd was on hand, there was much sharing of hymnals, but many knew the hymns so well that a hymnal was hardly necessary except for the words in the latter stanzas.

The other equipment items were fans. The fans were provided by the funeral director in Llano, and they were used only by the ladies. On one side of the cardboard (we called it "pasteboard") fan was a religious picture, such as Jesus wearing a crown of thorns; on the other side was the ad for Miles Buttery, funeral director and furniture dealer. The fans were considered community or church property, and they were left behind for other ladies to use.

Typically a meeting in those days began on Friday evening, but if a preacher of greater fame was conducting the meeting, it would run from one Sunday through the next Sunday. In our community, services were held twice daily on weekdays and three times on Sunday. Morning services during the week were like Sunday school classes, since the congregations consisted almost entirely of some elderly widows and their grandchildren too young to be useful at home. But the earnest minister was likely to be just as fervent with such a group, for he wanted to set the young people on the right path, and he knew better than to underestimate the influence of elderly widows on others in their households. But by the end of the Thirties, morning services during the week had stopped. Since the typical farmer, even though his crops were laid by, had plenty of things to do if he was at all diligent, he did not want to give up his mornings to going to church services. Generally there were no afternoon (we called them "evening") services except on Sundays.

Night services were another matter; they were held after the evening chores had been done. And there was something cosy about services at night. For one thing, since almost everyone there was local, there was a neighborly air about them. And not many of those who had not already professed their belief would be there. Sometimes there would be special music by a small local group who had been singing together. The preacher, unless he saw someone in the congregation who he felt was a potential candidate for conversion, was likely to be in a relaxed mood. He would joke a bit, but he would also preach an evangelical sermon, and he would make the invitation while the congregation sang such traditional songs as "Oh Why Not Tonight," "Just as I Am," or "Jesus Is Calling." And there was always the chance that there was someone present who could be proselytized. But there was often not quite the intensity of other services, although some preachers took these less emotional sessions as a time to reenforce some doctrinal points. More legalistic preachers would quote chapter and verse at some length to substantiate their positions.

The Sunday services were, of course, the big ones. The morning service ran from about eleven until shortly after noon, the afternoon service from about half past two until half past three. Usually there was a half hour or so of song service before the afternoon preaching. After the preaching, folks could go home and do the evening chores and get something to eat before the night service.

An important part of every meeting was someone to lead the singing. Dad usually led the singing for Church of Christ meetings, especially if one of my uncles was doing the preaching. In larger communities the person leading the singing was paid at least a small fee, but Dad would have been embarrassed to accept anything from the poor folk in our community. In fact, a local man who held meetings all summer to supplement his small income from cotton and pigs said he never asked for more than a few dollars besides his keep because he knew the folks could not afford it and he was more interested in saving souls than he was in making money.

A prime feature of the Sunday service was dinner on the grounds. When the tabernickle was built, a place for setting up the meal was also built. It was an open shed, at least thirty feet long and four feet wide, which had a board roof that provided shade for the long board table supported by posts. The food was placed on the table buffet style. There was always an abundance of home-raised food: fried chicken, cured pork, canned beef, fresh or home-canned garden products, and pies and cobblers from local canned peaches. Bakery bread and iced tea were provided by the members of the church holding the meeting. In the depth of the Depression there were families that stayed away from the Sunday morning sessions of meetings because they had no food they felt was good enough to take. I can recall one man telling my father they had not planned to attend until he killed two good-sized squirrels on Saturday afternoon.

While there were often flimsy paper plates available, most people brought dishes and flatware for others to use, exhibiting that unquestioning faith in the honesty of their fellows. Serving spoons which sometimes got switched from their original dishes had a way of finding their way home.

In the middle of the Depression, clothing was a problem, but no one would come to meetings in work clothes. Women wore shirtwaist dresses they had made themselves from flower print cloth. A few men had suits left from a more prosperous day just after World War I, but most came in shirt sleeves and "dress" pants, that is, pants made of any cloth except denim. Nearly all men would have on ties, but a few simply wore clean shirts buttoned at the neck. I never saw a man in church without socks, but I have seen more than one wearing socks with holes at the heels.

Since a large part of revival meetings was the socializing, especially before, during, and after dinner on the grounds, people came from communities over fifty miles away to see relatives and friends. Attending a meeting was a sure way of seeing all the local folk. While there was occasionally a greater show of affection among the women, a simple hand-shake was usually the sole physical contact, and the style of the handshake was a single downward motion. One of my uncles who often conducted the meetings caused confusion, for he had learned a side-to-side movement after he moved away. The talk, of course, was of family members and the usual concerns of farm folk. The women talked of canning, and chickens and turkeys, and sewing, and especially quilt-ings; the men of crop expectations and rain, and hopes for good prices for cotton and livestock.

The degree to which socializing was a part of attending meetings is evident by the fact that people often talked after the generator had been cut off and the area was in darkness except for automobile headlights. My own reasons for going were that there was nothing else to do and that there was always the chance that young Pat Mayes would be there with a sack of Golden Grain smoking tobacco and we could go down behind the big outcropping of granite just west of the tabernickle and smoke during the service while discussing the sexual potential of girls in the community. Pat weighed close

to three hundred pounds, and I did not reach a hundred before I was sixteen, so we were not the most macho adolescents in the community.

The second Sunday was the culmination of the meeting. The pattern was much the same as that of the first Sunday except for the baptizing that was held after the afternoon service. Only the Church of Christ and the Baptists held immersion baptizings, and these were generally held in the Little Llano River if there were any holes with the three or more necessary feet of water. On one occasion the Church of Christ group held a baptizing in Dreary Hollow on our farm. Privately Grandma objected strenuously, but she dared not object publicly for she knew that Grandpa (who was dead only a year) would have invited any group to use his creek. So she sat in her room with her back to the creek and dipped snuff vigorously. Dreary Hollow was fed by a spring, so there was water even in a dry year. But the hole needed cleaning out, so on Saturday afternoon Dad and I went down and cleared out the moss, tossed out the cow chips, and dug out the creek above the hole so that there was a good flow from the spring.

The evening service on the last night would have a relaxed air, particularly if a sizable number had been saved during the meeting. If eight or ten had been baptized, it was a highly successful meeting, and even more so if one or two had been proselytized from a rival sect. Preachers, however, were of their very nature fervent, and they were always happy to stay over for a baptizing on Monday if there were any last-minute converts.

The techniques of evangelistic preachers have been examined by Bill Clements and others, so I will limit my comments to saying that some preachers seemed more intent on winning people from other churches than on anything else. But I should add that a triumph almost as great as winning people from other denominations was bringing back into the fold someone who had been backsliding for years.

Finally, let me say that if I have sometimes seemed rather flip in my treatment of revival meetings, my attitudes may be the result of having four preachers and two song leaders in the family.

All photographs reproduced by permission of F. E. Abernethy.

The Olsen family home in Clifton, Texas.

PALMER OLSEN

Growing Up in Bosque County

Editor's note: Palmer Henry Olsen of Clifton, Bosque County, is a second-generation Texan, his father and mother both coming from Norway to Clifton in the early 1880s. Palmer grew up in Clifton, then got a civil engineering degree at Texas A&M, where he was an outstanding athlete. He served in both World War I and World War II. In World War II he received a personal citation for service to Norway from Crown Prince Olav and later served as a military governor in Germany. In 1919 he married Esther Swenson, who lived two doors down from him in Clifton, and they had two daughters. Esther died in 1981.

Palmer is ninety-two years old as of this writing. He is still lean and tough, gristle and bone, totin' no fat. He is a long-time and loyal member of the Texas Folklore Society and a regular contributor at its meetings. His themes deal with the many accumulations of a long and rich life, but the best of his stories are the tales of his green years in the mainly Norwegian community of Clifton during the early years of this twentieth century.

The Badger Fight

I can't remember the date, but late in 1903 or early 1904 an important personage was coming to Clifton. A badger fight in his honor was planned to be held in an open space between Fallis's saloon and the icehouse. Pat, our small black-and-white bulldog, was chosen to fight the badger. Two days beforehand, excitement and betting in Fallis's saloon mounted to astronomical heights. I often wondered later how a "smart" nine-year-old, as I was, could possibly have been fooled for so long. I didn't even wonder why the badger, confined in a large pine drygoods box, should have to fight with a heavy twenty-foot chain around his neck.

The big day arrived. After flowery praise of the visitor and a flamboyant expression of Clifton's privilege to honor its distinguished guest, Mayor G. J. Gibbs—he always had a big "chaw" of tobacco overflowing from the corners of his mouth and dripping in two nasty streams off the sides of his chin onto his pot belly—Mayor Gibbs handed the end of the chain to the guest and assured him that Clifton was conferring upon him its greatest honor. The guest was urged to make certain his pull on the chain was quick and forceful so the badger would surely get in the open where he could properly use his fighting talents.

Pat, being very cooperative, was straining at the leash, and his growls and frequent lunges left no doubt of his eagerness for the fray. For the uninitiated he provided as much interest and excitement as—and maybe more than—the boxed badger. Certainly his act could not have been better.

The climactic moment came. Two men hoisted the front of the big box, the greenhorn visitor jerked hard on the chain, and the porcelain thunder mug came bouncing out—to the chagrin of the visitor and the great amusement of the audience. Believe it or not, our Pat, in the true spirit of this ancient joke, tore into the pot and shook it as if life depended on his victory.

I was so interested in Pat and so flabbergasted by the "badger" that I probably fell into a trance. I have recollections of nothing else except a vague picture of much backslapping and loud laughs.

Wild Goose

In 1900 when I was about six years old, my younger brother Lawrence and I visited the farm of Uncle Kris and

Palmer Olsen in WWI.

Aunt Annie, two miles past Norse and ten miles from Clifton, Texas. Uncle Kris owned several milk cows, among which was one named Wild Goose. She was a small, blackish cow—probably a scrub jersey—with some brown hairs on her sides and belly, white foreshanks, and horns that curved inward. There was a good reason for her name. When the time came to calve, she took off like a wild goose and always sought the farthest, wildest, most rugged and inaccessible spot in the pasture. It was an area of rocky cliffs and dense scrub brush. Hog plums, a few black haw, shin oak, and sumac, together with briars and prickly pears, formed an almost impenetrable jungle.

During our visit, the time came again for Wild Goose to have a calf. She failed to show up on two successive evenings. Uncle Kris hitched a horse to the buggy, and invited Lawrence and me to come along to find the cow. We were strongly warned to stay in the buggy and keep quiet. We had already been told by our Aunt Annie that Wild Goose was mean and would tolerate no one but our uncle when the calf was young.

We followed the woods road up by the big hollow live oak and through the thick Spanish oak groves and the few cedars; meandered along the branch past the wheat field; turned right into the narrow lane between the field and the hay meadow; then slid and pitched over the ruts and gullies up the rougher, steeper road past the mountain tank; and finally weaved through the ever-thicker brush to the end of the road. Uncle Kris tied the horse to a small live oak and told us again to keep quiet and stay in the buggy. After an hour or so—it seemed ages to us—he returned leading Wild Goose, her small calf wobbling along behind. We reached the cow lot about sundown.

It was beginning to get dark when Uncle Kris started milking Wild Goose. Lawrence and I naturally wanted to miss no part of this wild cow operation, so, uninvited, we crawled upon the fence and sat down on the top plank. We had hardly settled when Wild Goose spotted us. She was standing broadside, and when she wheeled to come at us, she rolled Uncle

The author during WWII.

Kris over his stool and kicked the half-full milk bucket right in his face. Lawrence and I didn't stop to argue with Wild Goose or to make a dignified retreat. We fell backward off the fence and hit the ground running for the house. For reasons you can guess, that top plank remained ever after the hottest seat this side of Huntsville.

Uncle Kris kept that cow for years. Though Aunt Annie normally milked the cows, especially in busy harvests, she would never even come close to the cowpen for several weeks after Wild Goose had had a new calf. How much extra time and labor were lost because of that measly, almost worthless critter will never be known.

The Dancing Sons of Hermann

January 1, 1900, began a most instructive and wonderful year for me, a five-year-old, homegrown boy. I had been wearing dresses and had just gotten my first pair of pants. I also had just had my first haircut. My two older sisters wept long and bitterly when Mama sheared my shoulder-length crop of golden curly hair. My bonnets, both the plain and the Sunday-go-to-meeting kind with an overflow of flowery ruffles and ribbons, were discarded for new headgear—a plain cap and a fancy one, military style, with an ornament in front.

It was also the year that I first heard of the evils of dancing. In visits with my young friends to the Methodist and Presbyterian churches, I was told that dancing was the Devil's special handiwork to lure the young and the old into Hell. It was an awful contemplation. But, at fish fries or family parties, I had seen my mother dance and had heard her sing for hours the folk tunes of her native Norway. And I had heard or seen no devils. But, also, I knew of no dances in Clifton or of any desire for them.

A few years later, about 1906, the Sons of Hermann, a German fraternity, bought a small acreage in the edge of the woods bordering the prairie between the Bosque and Brazos rivers and built a clubhouse and dance hall. The area could be reached only by a very narrow cattle lane connected to the Clifton-to-Roswell road or over the bald prairie. Most of the dancers came ahorseback. The dancing to very lively music was a hopping, jerky kind of step. They were probably doing the polka. To Lawrence and me it was a very comical performance. As spectators only, we attended every dance and called the place The German Dude.

The dances at The German Dude had their interesting sidelights, one of which concerned a German friend of ours. Ernest Anz, a fiery and feisty young German, came ahorseback as usual to a dance one night. In the darkness his steed had trampled a skunk, and Ernest and his horse didn't smell like my lady's chamber. He was anxious to go to the dance and wondered if we had some perfume at our cousin's house that would mask the skunk odor. We assured him that we had nothing powerful enough for his purpose, and besides, we knew enough about skunk juice to know that nothing yet created—except maybe over-aged Limburger cheese—could neutralize his present odor. Ernest, disappointed and smelling bad, had to turn around and ride back home, danceless until the next gathering of Hermann's Sons.

Brown Derby Hats

On a Saturday evening in the spring of 1903, my father, who was in charge of the furniture department of P. E. Schow and Brothers general store in Clifton, sent word for his three older boys to come to the store at 8:00 P.M. We were ten, eight, and six years old. The day was a cool, fair day in a period of beautiful weather. At this time all stores stayed open till nine or later on Saturday evenings. Drugstores and grocery stores stayed open till eleven o'clock or sometimes as late as one o'clock on Sunday morning.

When we reached the store that evening our father took us into the dry-goods department and to our joy fitted us with brown derbies. No one today can understand or appreciate the feeling of a small boy being offered a *derby* to wear. Reaching manhood was the aim of every small boy, and wearing a derby was a real sign of having grown up. We were now Young Men.

Sunday morning continued the beautiful weather. We wore our derbies to church, as proud as any peacocks could strut. On Sunday afternoon, Dick Sedberry, our doctor's son, Sigurd Schow, and Herman Billert, son of a family friend, came to visit. And each boy wore a new brown derby hat! In our large backyard we began to play. Probably Herman—he was always full of mischief—began the game of "Popping Hats." If you never as a small boy enjoyed the game, you probably can't appreciate the sound or pleasure a child gets from popping a derby hat, of pushing in the top from the outside and then popping it out from the inside.

In no time at all, the derbies had no tops. Popping, both coming and going, had been too much. We now had only rims and hatbands. Strangely enough, I can't recall any whippings by our parents for this senseless hat destruction, so the fun undoubtedly far outweighed the agony of the rod or the loss of our precious and newly acquired hats. I'm sure we were punished, though. In those days "Spare the rod and spoil the child" was not merely a maxim; it was a prime law of every proud family.

The Elder and the Preacher's Son

In 1906 the Presbyterians of Clifton moved their church from just east of the Santa Fe railroad to the southwest corner of a lot several blocks west of the tracks and diagonally across H Avenue from our cane patch, and converted the building into a manse. A new church was built in the southeast corner of the narrow block.

W. M. Lewis was the new pastor. He had several children, including a young boy, Bill, about the same age as my brother Lawrence. They soon became fast friends and frequent companions. Bunk Swenson, another neighbor, soon made a close threesome. Often as a group they attended Rev. Lewis's church services, and prudently occupied a front seat

Palmer Olsen—ninety years old and still running.

next to Mr. R. L. Scott, the senior elder of the church. He always sat on the right end of the very front bench of the middle row of seats.

Bill was somewhat of a prankster, as most preachers' sons are reputed to be, and probably because of his frequent monkeyshines, he nearly always had to occupy a seat down front next to Mr. Scott. One Sunday, Bill had Lawrence and Bunk as guests and, maybe purposely, sat next to Elder Scott. Somehow Bill had obtained one of those little fascinating trick booklets whose covers depict a very beautiful and colorful Egyptian princess dressed in her eastern finery. Her rich and very scant raiment revealed all the charms of a female beauty. The booklet had one of those "come hither" titles that would have provoked anybody's curiosity. And, on this fine Sunday morning, Bill had brought his booklet to church.

About the time Rev. Lewis began his sermon, Bill sneaked his pretty booklet out onto his lap in a nonchalant way and seemingly gave his undivided attention to his father's sermon. The bright cover cast a gleam in Elder Scott's eyes and ruffled his solemn demeanor. Slyly he reached over and took the booklet from Bill's hands, secured it firmly with both fists in his lap, and resumed his sedate and apparent full attention to the sermon. After a few moments, however, he glanced down at the colorful picture and, seduced by his curiosity, opened the attractive volume. The result was a loud and devastating bang that made a smoking hell out of Elder Scott's serenity. He had no time to ponder or repent; he was a total disaster, as were that Sunday's services.

All photographs reproduced by permission of Palmer Olsen.

GUY LOGSDON

Cowboy Poets

As long as people eat beef there will be cowboys. As long as there are cowboys there will be cowboy poets, for cowboys love poetry. No other occupation has inspired as many poets as has the cattle industry, and in recent years these cowboy poets and reciters have been receiving long-deserved public attention. National, even international, attention is the result of the Annual Cowboy Poetry Gathering held in late January each year in Elko, Nevada.

This current public and scholarly interest in contemporary cowboy poets and reciters of poetry is a fascination with contradiction, for the cowboy is the epitome of masculinity, independent life-style, and freedom of thought and expression—the ideal American knight in shining armor. Poets have not enjoyed this image.

Cowboy poets have been out there for well over a century, but they have been ignored in favor of "singing cowboys." For decades the American public accepted the romantic image of the singing cowboy. Even the most masculine, strong, silent reel cowboy could be forgiven for a crude attempt at singing cowboy songs, but imagine the public reaction had John Wayne, Gary Cooper, or even Gene Autry been pictured writing poems and reciting poetry. Today, the real cowboy is getting recognition, for cowboys wrote and recited far more poetry than songs.

Numerous individuals and organizations were involved in planning and producing the First Gathering, January 31– February 2, 1985, but the dominant idea and voice for the gathering came from James Griffith, Director of the South-west Folklore Center at the University of Arizona, Tucson. His friendship with Van Holyoke, an Arizona cowboy singer, poet, and reciter, made him aware of the poetry-recitation traditions and the lack of interest folklorists gave to them. Also, Griffith had studied the life and poetry of another cowboy poet friend, Everett Brisendine of Chino Valley, Arizona.[1] Griffith's determination, combined with that of Hal Cannon, Director of the Western Folklife Center in Salt Lake City, brought together many state folklorists. Their combined energies created the 1985 meeting, but the gathering required a general definition of cowboy poetry. The definition written by Mike Korn, Montana State Folklorist, became the guideline.

> Cowboy Poetry is rhymed, metered verse written by someone who has lived a significant portion of his or her life in Western North American cattle culture. The verse reflects an intimate knowledge of that way of life, and the community from which it maintains itself in tradition. Cowboy poetry may or may not in fact be anonymous in authorship but must have qualities, content and style which permit it to be accepted into the repertoire of the cultural community as reflecting that community's aesthetics in style, form and content.
>
> The structural style of cowboy poetry has its antecedents in ballad style of England and the Appalachian South. It is similar to popular works of authors such as Robert W. Service and Rudyard Kipling.[2]

It was during the Third Gathering that I listened to two poets discuss poetry and learned what cowboy poetry is. Late in the evening of January 29, 1987, Baxter and Cindy Black, Wallace "Wally" McRae, and I were finishing dinner in the BilTo'Ki "The Gathering Place," the Basque American Dinner House, when Baxter leaned forward across the table and asked Wally, "What is it like to write 'Reincarnation,' the ultimate cowboy poem—a poem with universal appeal?"

We had enjoyed an evening of excellent food, laced with "room temperature cheap red wine" and conversation. Baxter Black is a Colorado cowman-veterinarian-turned-poet, who now makes his living as a poet, columnist, humorist, and after-dinner entertainer. Wally McRae is a third-generation Montana rancher and a first-generation poet; in 1986 he and his family celebrated the one hundredth anniversary of their family ranch. Also, in 1975 or 1976 he wrote "Reincarnation" (first published in 1979) which is rapidly becoming a standard poem in reciters' repertories.

"What does reincarnation mean?"
A cowpoke ast his friend.
His pal replied, "It happens when
Yer life has reached its end.
They comb yer hair, and warsh yer neck,
And clean yer fingernails,
And lay you in a padded box
Away from life's travails."

"The box and you goes in a hole
That's been dug into the ground.
Reincarnation starts in when
Yore planted 'neath a mound.
Them clods melt down, just like yer box,
And you who is inside.
And then yore just beginnin' on
Yer transformation ride."

"In a while, the grass'll grow
Upon yer rendered mound.
'Till some day on yer moldered grave
A lonely flower is found.
And say a hoss should wander by,
And graze upon this flower,
That once wuz you, but now's become
Yer vegetative bower."

"The posey that the hoss done ate
Up, with his other feed,
Makes bone, and fat, and muscle
Essential to the steed.
But some is left that he can't use,
And so it passes through,
And finally lays upon the ground.
This thing, that once wuz you."

"Then say, by chance, I wanders by
And sees this upon the ground,
And I ponders, and I wonders at,
This object that I found.
I thinks of reincarnation,
Of life, and death, and such
I come away concludin': Slim,
You ain't changed, all that much." [3]

Baxter caught Wally off guard with his question, but after a few seconds of thought, Wally offered a reply.

McRAE: I don't think about it. It was the easiest poem I ever wrote. I have three or four that I like better than that one. I'm surprised that they [reciters] do it. In fact, I think, maybe, it's overdone. It's a superficial poem; I don't know what the attraction is.

BLACK: That poem is acceptable anywhere, in an English class. It will be in classic collections. Look at the words. I would never think of "vegetative bower," but *you* think in those terms. YOU WRITE WITH YOUR *BRAIN*, not just emotion!

McRAE: It wrote itself. I didn't look it up in a thesaurus. And "posey" is not a very erudite word. Actually, it gestated for about two years. I heard the story told as a Jewish joke, but the man didn't have a good accent. He tried to use a Brooklyn accent, which was funnier than the joke. And I got the line "comb your hair, wash your neck, and clean your fingernails" from the song in the musical *Oklahoma!*, "Poor Jud Is Dead."

One evening it came to me, so I sat down, and I grafted and adapted. I wrote it in a half hour.

BLACK: How do you write your poems? Lately, I'm getting wrapped up in the technique of it. I'm striving for perfect meter and perfect rhyme!

McRAE: Well, I have it in my mind before writing it down. It has to be in meter, in rhyme, in stanzas, and I try to have the last stanza so I don't wander too much. And I strike out the meter by hand and write the meter in the upper right-hand corner of the paper. You know, I've printed poems that I *still* don't like all the words in them. I have more ideas than I have poems. You have all kinds of emotional levels in your poetry; your poems *always* have an underlying truth.

BLACK: I write to perform, not to read. I build my audience up; then I always have a line to let the air out. I take them off the hook, except in "A Time To Stay, A Time To Go."

> Ya know, I got this ranch from my daddy
> He come here in seventeen
> He carved this place outta muscle and blood;
> His own and his ol' 'percheon' team.
>
> I took over in fifty
> And married my darlin' in May.
> Together we weathered whatever came up
> She had what it took to stay.
>
> Last winter we finally decided
> We'd pack up and leave in the spring.
> The kids are all grown and 'city-folk,' now;
> We never raised 'em to cling.
>
> Oh sure, I wished they'd have wanted
> To ranch and carry it on
> But they did their part, I thank 'em fer that
> And they chose. Now all of 'em's gone.
>
> The last thirty odd years we've collected
> An amazing number of things!

Bonnets and bottles, clippings and letters
And Dad's ol' surcingle rings.

We've spent the winter months sorting.
Our hearts would ache or would jump
As we looked at our lives in trinkets we'd saved
Then boxed up or took to the dump.

We cried sometimes in the attic
I'm not ashamed of the truth.
I love this ol' ranch that we're leavin'
We gave it the strength of our youth.

I love this ol' woman beside me
She held me and stayed by my side.
When I told 'er I's thinkin' 'bout sellin'
She said, "Honey, I'm here for the ride."

These new fellers movin' in Monday
Are nice and I wish 'em good luck.
But I'd rather be gone, so Ma, git yer stuff
I've already gassed up the truck.

Lookin' back over my shoulder
At the mailbox I guess that I know
There's a time to be stayin', a time to be goin'
And I reckon it's time that we go.[4]

BLACK: I don't use it now. I wrote it because there were old
couples who left their ranches and farms for the right reason.
Now I don't use it, 'cause it hurts my friends.
MCRAE: You don't write anything that's bitter.
BLACK: What about "Food Is For People, Not Profit!"?[5]
MCRAE: Naw, Hell, I write bitter. I have a killer instinct.
Those sons-a-bitches [strip miners] taught me well; my "Things
of Intrinsic Worth" reflects it.

Remember that sandrock on Emmells Crick
Where Dad carved his name in 'thirteen?
It's been blasted down into rubble,

And interred by their dragline machine.
Where Fadhls lived, at the old Milar Place,
Where us kids stole melons at night?
They 'dozed it up in a funeral pyre
Then torched it. It's gone alright.
The "C" on the hill, and the water tanks
Are now classified, "reclaimed land."
They're thinking of building a golf course
Out there, so I understand.
The old Egan Homestead's an ash pond,
That they say is eighty feet deep.
And the branding corral at the Douglas Camp
Is underneath a spoil heap;
And across the creek is a tipple, now
Where they load coal onto a train.
And my folks' "Miller Coulee Homestead"
Is no more . . . except in my brain.
There's a railroad loop and a coal storage shed
Where the bison kill-site used to be.
The Guy Place is gone. And Ambrose's too.
Beulah Farley's a ranch refugee.

But things are booming. We got this new school
That's envied by the whole state.
When folks up and ask, "How's things goin' down there?"
I grin like a fool and say, "Great!"
Great God, how we're doin'! We're rollin' in dough,
As they tear and they ravage the Earth.
And nobody knows, or nobody cares
About things of intrinsic worth.[6]

  As Wally spoke the last line, our eyes were moist, and
there was momentary silence. Baxter with emotional admiration said; "Do you know you suck people up into that? You
don't write with your brain!" With modesty Wally replied,
"Sometimes I do."
  The conversation continued with Baxter turning the
emotional tables by reciting an epic poem, "The Buckskin

Montana rancher and poet Wallace McRae. *Courtesy of Wallace McRae.*

Cowboy poet Baxter Black. *Courtesy of Baxter Black.*

Curley Fletcher—most widely sung and recited of cowboy poets. *From the Collection of Guy Logsdon.*

Jack Thorp—cowboy poet and the first known collector of cowboy songs and poetry. *From the Collection of Guy Logsdon.*

Mare," which he had finished that afternoon. "I want to try it with you." The theme was a cowboy's conflict with a wild mustang mare that resulted in the cowboy's mental destruction; then Wally wiped away the moisture with "You son-of-a-bitch, you got me."

For me, the evening was one of awe and inspiration, listening to a rancher who writes and speaks with love for his land and heritage, and to a wandering cowman who travels the nation writing and speaking with love, concern, and humor for all people.

Cowboy poetry has traditionally been tagged as doggerel, verse, or mere rhymes. However, as with all poetry through the ages, there are excellent as well as far-from-excellent poems. But the cowboy writes and recites for cowboys, not literary acclaim, and the measure of success is when cowboys absorb a poem into their traditional culture.

An early attempt to include cowboy poetry in the large body of American poetry came from Alice Corbin Henderson. As Associate Editor of the influential periodical *Poetry: A Magazine of Verse*, she devoted the August 1920 (Vol. XVI, No. V) issue to western poetry and included eight cowboy poems by N. Howard "Jack" Thorp. However, she used the title "Cowboy Songs" and throughout the issue referred to cowboy poems as songs, which seemed to rationalize her interest. In fact, Henderson relegated most regional poets to "folk-poetry" or "songs," or songs (poems) " . . . of purely native origin and owing little or nothing to an inherited literary tradition." She was at least kind in criticisms; others have been less kind.

Western collectors and writers John A. Lomax and J. Frank Dobie had strong classical literature foundations and passed judgment on cowboy poetry as being mostly doggerel. Lomax revised, edited, expurgated, and bowdlerized his collected songs and compiled one collection of poetry, *Songs of the Cattle Trail and Cow Camp* (Macmillan Company, 1919). In the "Introduction" he qualified the contents as " . . . attempts, more or less poetic, in translating scenes connected with the life of a cowboy." While a few selections were anonymous, most poets were identified: James Barton Adam, Larry Chittenden, Arthur Chapman, Charles Badger Clark, Jr., Henry Herbert Knibbs, and many more. Lomax received the poems from cowboys and individuals interested in cowboy culture. At least he appreciated the fact that poetry was popular among working cowboys.

Dobie was far less kind. In his *Guide to Life and Literature of the Southwest*, Dobie devoted a chapter to "Poetry and Drama." He stated:

> No poor poetry is worth reading. Taste for the best makes the other kind insipid.
>
> Compared with America's best poetry, most poetry of the Southwest is as mediocre as American poetry in the mass is as compared with the great body of English poetry between Chaucer and Masefield.[7]

Dobie listed a few poets of merit, mostly from the Santa Fe/Taos literary colony, and he gave qualified praise to Eugene Manlove Rhodes's poem, "The Hired Man on Horseback." It is

> a long poem of passionate fidelity to his own decent kind of men, with power to ennoble the reader, and with the form necessary to all beautiful composition. This is the sole and solitary piece of poetry to be found in all the myriads of rhymes classed as "cowboy poetry."[8]

Rhodes may have spoken to Dobie, but not to the working cowboy, as the first stanza indicates. Few, if any, cowboys learn it for bunkhouse recitation:

Harp and flute and violin, throbbing through the night,
Merry eyes and tender eyes, dark head and bright;
Moon shadow on the sundial to mark the moments fleet,
The magic and enchanted hours where moonlight lovers meet;
And the harp notes come all brokenly by night winds stirred—
But the hired man on horseback is singing to the herd![9]

The cattle industry's major bibliographer, Ramon Adams, did not include poetry in his monumental bibliography, *The Rampaging Herd*. Very few writers have consumed cowboy culture as did Adams, but he wrote off poetry and songs with a short statement:

> I have purposely omitted books on cowboy songs, cowboy poetry. . . . These, I feel, do not belong to the range cattle industry, and would only add to the printing costs.[10]

Among the bookmen, bibliographers, and writers of the cowboy's culture, Louis P. Merrill stands out as the individual who was aware of what the cattle people read and enjoyed. He made no literary value judgments in his *Aristocrats of The Cow Country*. He listed and annotated the best and the rarest of the cow country books and provided a fine description of reading and books in the ranch house.

The reading habit among livestock producers, particularly the men and women of the cattle country, is much more pronounced than in any other segment of America's rural society. As a matter of fact, it probably equals or exceeds that of any group outside of the professions. It is possible to account for this in a measure by isolation, or seasonal leisure, or the highly complex nature of the range livestock production and management which requires an unusual stock of basic information in addition to current trends of economics and weather.

Not only is it significant that cowfolks read much, they like most to read about their own country. This is probably because the occupation they were born in represents an epoch in America unlike anything before or since. An occupation further from common experience than any other with customs having the force of law, its own standards of conduct, its own philosophy and lore.

Ranch headquarters are noted for sizeable libraries of good books, well used but well cared for. . . . [11]

Seven books of poetry, along with additional books that contain a few poems, were included among his one hundred "aristocrats." The poets were James Barton Adams, William Lawrence "Larry" Chittenden, Wallace D. Coburn, Nathan Kirk Griggs, F. W. La Frentz, N. Howard "Jack" Thorp, and C. C. Walsh, but not all were cowboys. Instead, they wrote about the cow country experiences through the eyes of the observer.

Merrill believed "Larry" Chittenden's *Ranch Verses* (G. P. Putnam's Sons, 1893) to be the "first book of poems on the range," a belief that I held until recently. While reading through volumes of poetry in my collection as well as those obtained through interlibrary loan services, I discovered that L. (Lysius) Gough privately published *Western Travels and Other Rhymes* (Dallas: A. D. Aldridge & Co.) in 1886. Gough wrote poems while cowboying in Texas in 1882 through 1884; he wrote about "actual life on the trail and ranch." As a result of his friends' encouragement, Gough had one thousand copies printed. It must have been a small, paperbound volume that easily fell apart. Of course critics, upon reading the poems, might assume that they were easily and readily discarded. I have seen only a photocopy of the title page as reprinted in his *Spur Jingles and Saddle Songs* (Amarillo, Texas: Russell Stationery Company, 1935).

In this paperbound collection Gough reprinted many of his ranch life poems and included the date they were written along with the events that inspired the poem. It is a valuable collection of reminiscences and experiences; however, it is impossible to speculate about Gough's popularity among cowboys or to assume that any of his poems entered oral tradition. In his 1935 volume, one poem, "Damn Fool" written February 5, 1883, is in the "Come all ye" tradition and is similar in theme to the folk song "Bad Companions." It contains thirteen verses of which I include the first, the fifth, and the thirteenth.

> Come all you young boys who long the west to see,
> Come listen to my story and warning take from me;
> And never while in youth do you attempt to roam;
> For you can never find a place like your father's home.

> I longed to be a cowboy, to work upon the trail,
> And face the cold stormy rains, also the snow and hail.
> For the life a cowboy I surely thought it best,
> And onward I traveled to the country of the west.

> So come all you young boys, be you rich or poor,
> Never start to rambling, 'twill teach you a lesson sure,
> Though you can ramble for twenty years or more,
> You will never find a place like your father's door.

I have read collections published prior to Gough's that contain no cowboy songs or poems; even though Francis D. Allan's *Allan's Lone Star Ballads* (Galveston: J. D. Sawyer, 1874) contains songs sung by cowboys, they are southern songs. The other collection, *Songs of the Southwest* (Topeka, Kansas: George W. Crane & Co., 1881), is the poetry of Theodore F. Price, "The Dramatic Impersonator"; these poems are vast in territory and subjects covered but do not include cowboys. Probably there are other small volumes printed before the Chittenden collection appeared, but I have not found them.

The standard method of transmission other than recitation was for local newspapers and livestock journals to print poems left at their office or mailed to them. Many poems were "anonymous," which is in part the result of the cowboy's fear of rejection, criticism, and ridicule or his general lack of self-confidence in poetry skills.

A few years ago, I searched the *Cheyenne Transporter* for other information and serendipitously found three cowboy poems. This semi-monthly newspaper was published at Darlington, Cheyenne and Arapaho Reservation, Indian Territory, from December 5, 1879, to August 12, 1886. Cattle drives, primarily following the Chisholm Trail, passed near Darlington; therefore, the newspaper carried much information from and about the men on the drives. The poems probably did not enter the repertory of the cowboy. However, "The Cowboy" in the November 5, 1884, issue is an interesting description of that breed of men.

> What is it has no fixed abode,
> Who seeks adventures by the load—
> An errant knight without a code?
>> The cowboy.
>
> Who finds it pleasure, cows to punch,
> When he would a whole "herd" bunch—
> Who ready for a fine grass lunch?
>> The cowboy.
>
> Who is it paints the town so red,
> And in the morning has a head
> Upon him like a feather bed?
>> The cowboy.
>
> Who is it with unbounded skill
> Will shoot big bullets with a will
> That generally has the effect to kill?
>> The cowboy.
>
> Who is it after all, who make
> Town trade good, and uniformly take
> For big hearts, what is called "the cake"?
>> The cowboy.

The front page of the last issue, August 12, 1886, carried "The Cowboy's Lament" (also known as "The Campfire Has Gone Out") in which the demise of the trail herd cowboy was reflected.

> Through progress of railroads,
> Our occupations gone,

We put our ideas into words,
　　Our words into a song.
First comes the cowboy,
　　He's pointed for the west;
Of all the pioneers I claim
　　The cowboy is the best.
We miss him on the round up;
　　Gone is his merry shout.
The cowboy's left the country,
　　And the campfire's going out.

There are three additional verses dedicated to the cowboy and the freighter—both displaced by the railroad. Also,
on March 25, 1882, an advertisement for Kahn and Schloss,
"Stockmen's Headquarters" for clothing in Kansas City, Mis-
souri, included a twenty-four-line poem, "The Stockman." It
emphasized that after the roundup and the cattle shipped east,
the stockmen gathered at Kahn and Schloss to visit, trade,
and purchase clothes. This poem-advertisement indicates
that poetry caught the eye of the cowboys.

　　Another serendipitous find, "A Cattle Stampede in the
Territory," appeared in *Twin Territories: The Indian Magazine*,
May 1904. This journal was published in Muskogee, Indian
Territory, for the Indians of Indian Territory and Oklahoma
Territory. The "Cattle Stampede" occurred in 1879, north of
the Cimarron River, when lightning, thunder, and heavy
hailstones made fifteen hundred head of IXL Texas cattle
"moan" and run. Unlike other "stampede" poems and songs,
no brave cowboy lost his life.

　　Untold numbers of scrapbooks and clipping collections
of cowboy poetry gathered from newspapers and popular journals have been thrown out by the children and grandchildren
of old-timers.

　　Many of the newspaper and journal poems were anonymous, and most did not become cowboy favorites. However,
the identity of the poet is known for many of the songs and
poems collected in cowboy traditional lore, and they were

written as poems, not songs. Larry Chittenden wrote "The Cowboys' Christmas Ball"; N. Howard "Jack" Thorp scratched out "Little Joe, the Wrangler" on a piece of brown paper in 1898; D. J. "Kid" O'Malley wrote "Charlie Rutledge," "When the Work's All Done This Fall," and "The Tenderfoot"; Charles Badger Clark, Jr., gave us "High-Chin Bob," "A Border Affair," and "A Cowboy's Prayer"; and more recently Gail I. Gardner added "The Sierry Petes" to traditional cowboy lore.[12] These represent only a few of the poem/songs of well-known cowboy poets. However, Curley W. Fletcher is the poet most widely recited and sung by working cowboys.

Fletcher was a California-Nevada cowboy who had prolific writing skills and the ability to tell a story in a colorful, concise style. His "Strawberry Roan" was anonymously set to music and became one of the most popular cowboy ballads to be sung. Other Fletcher poems that became songs include "The Wild Buckaroo," "Ridge Runnin' Roan," and "The Flyin' U Twister" or "Bad Brahma Bull." His poems that entered cowboy recitation tradition include "Cowboy's Soliloquy," "The Sheep-herder's Lament," and "The Open Ledger," which is the classic bawdy cowboy poem. Fletcher did not hesitate to take advantage of the cowboy's love of bawdry. His "The Open Ledger," also known as "The Open Book," is a humorous, bawdy description of the specific characteristics of cowboys in each state; Fletcher more than adequately refuted the cowboy myth. Also, he wrote his own bawdy parodies of "The Wild Buckaroo" and "The Strawberry Roan." In fact, "The Castration of the Strawberry Roan" is probably the most widely sung bawdy cowboy song.[13]

Another well-loved cowboy poet was Bruce Kiskaddon, who cowboyed in Colorado and Arizona before becoming a bellhop in Los Angeles. His poems were widely distributed throughout the West in the 1930s and 1940s by the Los Angeles Union Stock Yards; each month they published a "Monthly Livestock Letter" and for many years included a Kiskaddon poem. My incomplete run (twenty-nine issues) of "Letters" starts with June 1936 and ends with April 1944.

Old-time cowboys say that "he wrote it the way it was."[14]

By no means is this essay more than a superficial introduction to cowboy poets, past and present. My longtime interest in cowboy songs and books motivated me through the
years to pick up many poetry books in used-book stores. At
the present, I have over one hundred titles. The Fife Collection at Utah State University contains many more, and in
other privately owned collections I have seen titles that were
privately published for family and friends. This does not take
into account the vast numbers published in newspapers and
journals. As self-criticism, I confess that I do not own a Carlos Ashley book;[15] yet, I learned "Bob Sear's Chili Joint" from
Baxter Black. To know an Ashley poem, but not to own his
book, is what cowboy poetry and recitation are all about.

Notes

1. James S. Griffith, "The Cowboy Poetry of Everett Brisendine: A
   Response to Cultural Change," Western Folklore 42 (January 1983):
   38–45.
2. This was a typed statement in a packet of materials mailed to the
   1985 planning committee. For a sampling of the First Gathering see
   Hal Cannon, ed., Cowboy Poetry: A Gathering (Salt Lake City: Peregrine Smith Books, 1985).
3. Copyright 1986 by Wallace McRae. Reprinted by permission of the
   author and the publisher from Wallace McRae, It's Just Grass and
   Water (Spokane, Wash.: The Oxalis Group, 1986), pp. 28–29. Another collection of McRae's poetry is Up North Is Down The Crick
   (Bozeman, Mont.: Museum of the Rockies, 1985).
4. Copyright 1986 by Baxter Black. Reprinted by permission of the
   author and the publisher from Baxter Black, Coyote Cowboy Poetry
   (Denver: Record Stockman Press, 1986), p. 80. Also, Black has five
   additional books of poetry and newspaper articles, all available from
   the Coyote Cowboy Company, Brighton, Colo., 80601.
5. See Black, Coyote Cowboy Poetry, p. 170.

6. Copyright by Wallace McRae. This unpublished poem was given to me in manuscript form and is reprinted here by permission of the author.

7. J. Frank Dobie, *Guide to Life and Literature of the Southwest* (Dallas: Southern Methodist University Press, 1952), p. 184.

8. Ibid., p. 185.

9. May Davison Rhodes, *The Hired Man On Horseback* (Boston: Houghton Mifflin Company, 1938), pp. ix–xiii.

10. Ramon Adams, *The Rampaging Herd* (Norman: University of Oklahoma Press, 1959), p. xviii.

11. Louis P. Merrill, *Aristocrats of The Cow Country* (Eagle Pass, Tex.: Pack-Saddle Press, 1973), p. 4.

12. For information about these poets and songwriters, see John I. White, *Git Along, Little Dogies* (Urbana: University of Illinois Press, 1975) and N. Howard "Jack" Thorp, *Songs of the Cowboys* (Lincoln: University of Nebraska Press, 1984), Foreword by Guy Logsdon.

13. Hal Cannon has written a concise biographical sketch in his Preface to Curley Fletcher, *Songs of the Sage* (Salt Lake City: Peregrine Smith Books, 1986). In reference to bawdy cowboy songs, my manuscript of songs that I have collected will be published under the title "The Whorehouse Bells Were Ringing and Other Songs Sung By Cowboys" by the University of Illinois Press.

14. Hal Cannon edited and wrote the Introduction to a new collection of Kiskaddon poems, *Rhymes of the Ranges* (Salt Lake City: Peregrine Smith Books, 1987).

15. Carlos Ashley's *That Spotted Cow and Other Texas Hill Country Ballads* (Austin: Shoal Creek Publishers, 1975) has been published at least two times since 1941; he has been the "Dean" of Texas cowboy poets as well as the Poet Laureate of Texas. Texas cowboy poets who have attended the Cowboy Poetry Gathering include Buster McLaury, Guthrie; Sam Brown, Adrian; and Joel and Barney Nelson, Alpine. Also, the first Texas Cowboy Poetry Gathering was held in Alpine, March 6–7, 1987, and other states have held or plan to hold similar gatherings.

ELTON MILES

Folk Poetry
Texas, Southwest

Presented in this paper are sixteen poems that might or might not be real folk poetry, if such lore is restricted to oral repetition and consequent variation. Yet, when somebody just ups and writes a string of doggerel, shares copies with friends, or fires it off to a newspaper, he and his performance are of the folk.

Pertaining to Texas and the Southwest, these poems span more than a hundred years and range in topic from buffalo hunting to the seat belt. They are all folk productions, with only one, it seems, partly in the oral tradition. Like the oral, they imitate existing forms and speak in conventional poetic idiom, warping rhythm and rhyme for the sake of plain speaking. Unlike their oral counterparts, they resist variation and often preserve an author's identity. Few become so widely known as "Lasca." Many, as in the oral tradition, are obscene.

These few owe their survival to those appreciative souls who hoarded them. Hoarding them is possible only because of writing, the printing press, typewriter, mimeograph, and photocopy machine. They crop up in bureau drawers and account books. Copies are passed by hand among friends, sometimes copied again and shared through the U.S. Mail. (This article itself is a copying and a sharing.)

The Buffalo Hunters

For generations the newspaper has provided a multi-copy medium through which the folk poet may perform. Sometimes the writer seems shy about performing in public print, but with or without some reluctance allows a friend to see to the poem's publication. Such is the case with "The Buffalo Hunters." Upon its appearance in an 1878 Kansas newspaper, these words appeared beneath the title: "Respectfully Ascribed to Harry Baker by Rambling Jim."

Because the buffalo hunter's trade on the Texas plains provided the same work-social environment as it did anyplace else, this Dodge City poem applied as well to Fort Griffin or Sweetwater, Texas. It is rich with details of the hunt, camp life, and the hunter's attitude toward the skinners, the buyers, and other plains types. Conventionally, it concludes with the rambling man's dream of settling down, a dream diluted with nostalgia for the hunt.

The poem observes a syncopated couplet, with lines ranging from four to seven stresses, mainly iambic, perhaps eight in the last. Often the number of stresses to the line is at the discretion of the reciter, depending on how he chooses to bunch words together.[1]

Here is what Elmer Kelton rescued from oblivion in his *Pioneer News-Observer*, 1974.

Of all the lives beneath the sun
The buffalo hunter's is the jolliest one.
His wants few, simple and easily supplied,
A wagon, team, gun, and a horse to ride,
He chases the buffalo o'er the plains;
A shot at smaller game he disdains.
Bison hides are his bills of exchange,
And all are his that come within range.
From the wintry blast they shield his form
And afford him shelter during the storm.
A steak from the hump is a feast for a king;
Brains, you know, are good and tongue a delicious thing;
When the day's hunt is over and all have had their dinners,
The hunter lights his pipe to entertain the skinners.
He tells of the big bull that bravely met his fate,

Of the splendid line shot that settled his mate,
Of the cow, shot too low, of another too high,
And of all shots that missed he tells the reason why,
How the spike stood his ground when all but him had fled
And refused to give it up till he filled him full of lead,
How he trailed up the herd for five miles or more,
Leaving over forty victims weltering in their gore.
All about the blasted calves that put the main herd to flight
And kept them on the run until they disappeared from sight.
When weary of incidents relating to the chase,
They discuss other topics, each one in its place—
Law, politics, religion and the weather,
And the probable price of buffalo leather.
A tender-footed hunter is a great greenhorn,
And the poor old granger an object of scorn,
But the worst deal of all is reserved for hide buyers,
Who are swindlers and robbers and professional liars.
The hunter thinks sometimes in the future of a change in his
    life,
And indulges in dreams of a home and a wife
Who will sit by his side and listen to a story
    of the boys and the past
And echo his hopes of reunion in the happy
    hunting grounds at last.[2]

When the Jackass Learns to Sing Tenor

This untitled, one-sentence string of eight couplets written in 1928 served the anonymous writer in expressing his
locally shared political opinion in Coryell County, Texas.
Consistent throughout is a parallel structure of phrasing. It
was typed on a gelatin stencil, apparently to make two copies
per mimeographed sheet, thus economizing on paper.

In the 1980s I found a copy on a half-sheet among the
tax receipts of my late grandfather, H. J. Rogers, cotton and
subsistence farmer near Levita. This half-sheet had been

folded so as to fit into the long, snap-top purse in which he carried his greenbacks.

Humorously, this poem echoes the rural Texas hostility against presidential candidate Al Smith. Under an arbor I heard a preacher rail against Al because of his wish to repeal the Eighteenth Amendment. These verses do not mention the demon, rum; one line, however, suggests fear of Catholic influence, also harped on by the preacher.

Mainly this work produces earthy images from folk language to illustrate the impossibility of Al Smith's ever winning the presidency. Most of the syncopated lines have three stresses, some of them four.

> When the Jackass learns to sing Tenor,
> And the Rattle Snake walks on legs,
> When the Razor Back Hog grows feathers,
> And the Milk Cow sets on eggs,
> When the Blue Bird mates with the Wood Pecker,
> And the Cat Owl mates with the hens,
> When the Bull Frog sails with swany wings
> And the Sap Sucker chums with the Wrens,
> When cotton grows on Fig trees,
> And apples spring from the Rose,
> When the Catholics rule the United States,
> And a Jew grows a real straight nose,
> When Pope Pius is head of the Ku Klux Klan,
> In the land of Uncle Sam,
> Then Al Smith will be President of this country,
> And it won't be worth a damn.

A Big Fish Story

What little history there is to "A Big Fish Story" illustrates how a folk poem in print expands the audience of a folk poet's performance. When it appeared in a 1933 *Coryell County News*, the editor's note said: "The following poem was brought to the *News* office by Gene Hodges. It was published in the *Hamilton County News* recently, a copy of which was sent to Mr. and Mrs. Hodges by their daughter. The poem was a contribution of Rev. S. A. Rains to the *Hamilton County News.*" Beneath the title the Gatesville paper ascribed authorship, "By Rev. S. A. Rains."

Next, my grandfather read it, apparently tore the page out, and stowed it in his trunk with other personal papers (including the previous poem). After he died in the late 1930s, it went into my mother's keepsakes. It traveled with my parents from Waco to Brownwood and back to Gatesville, where it ended up with me when they thinned out their papers. Neither my grandfather nor my parents had ever heard of folk poetry, but they knew what they liked.

The poem expresses the feeling and thought of the group in which Brother Rains was a leader, that of rural Texas Protestantism of his time. Its lively storytelling is in keeping with traditions of his people. It presents a Baptist country minister's Biblical knowledge and a jocularity as well as a doctrine of salvation shared by his flock. When I was a small boy, Brother Rains was my grandparents' pastor at Levita, and I remember him as a tall, heavyset jovial man who loved children and made it pleasant for us to be around him.

Basically, he formed his poem in four-beat Hudibrastic couplets, a form much adapted to satire by many literary poets. In this case, the dominant foot is anapestic rather than iambic. Below, paragraph divisions are imposed, as there are none in the original.

A Bible lesson learned while in my youth
Is a big fish story, but every word the truth.
Just listen now and I'll tell you the tale,
How Jonah, the prophet, got caught by the whale.

Jonah had sinned and strayed from the fold:
A big fish caught him and swallowed him whole.
Now a part of the story is awfully sad
For the city of Ninevah had gone to the bad;
The Lord looked down on their wicked ways

In hopes of repentance in forty more days;
The Lord called Jonah, but Jonah said "no!
I'm a hardshell preacher and I will not go;
Those people in Ninevah are nothing to me;
I'm no foreign missionary and never will be."
So Jonah started to Tarshish in greatest haste
Boarding a ship bound for that place;
But God looked down, so the Bible records,
And spied old Jonah running from the Lord;
So God started a wind, endangering the sail,
And the efforts of Jonah began to fail;
The ship began rocking, was tossed by the way;
Then old Jonah was sorry he did not obey.
He confessed it was caused by his awful sin.
The crew threw him over—the fish took him in.

The fish said to Jonah, "old fellow, don't fret
I came to take you in out of the wet;
You are going to be punished for your awful sin."
And he opened his mouth and old Jonah went in;
So the funniest sight that ever was seen
Was Jonah going off in this new submarine.
Well, the city of Ninevah delayed to repent,
The message of warning to them was mis-sent.
On the beds of the sea the old fish sought rest,
He had swallowed food that would not digest,
So he got mighty restless and was sorely afraid.
For he rumbled inside when the old prophet prayed;
So God's message of warning to Ninevah lays
In a dead letter office through nights and days;
The old prophet was shut in as tight as a lock,
But the Lord will open as sure as you knock.

The old prophet was down on his face
Praying in anguish to get out of that place.
On the third day the fish arose from his bed,
Sick at his stomach, with a pain in his head,

And he said to himself, "I must have air quick,
For this old sinner is making me sick."
So he opened his eyes and wiggled his tail
And pulled for the shore to deliver his mail.
When he got to the shore he looked all around,
Then vomited old Jonah clear out on the ground.

Then Jonah thanked God for His mercy and grace
And looked at the whale with a great long face;
He then gazed round with a wistful eye,
Sat down in the sunshine, his clothes for to dry.
He thought what a power his preaching would be,
Just from a whale seminary a prophet set free.
After resting himself and being dried by the sun,
He set out for Ninevah as hard as he could run;
He said to himself, "I will never more sin,
For if I should I'd get swallowed again."

So he arrived at the city about four days late,
But he began preaching when he entered the gate;
He told them the message that God said tell,
And urged them to repent that they might miss hell.
They heard his message, repented and prayed,
And the hand of justice from them was stayed.

But Jonah got mad when God saved the town,
Went off in the woods, sat down on the ground;
So God caused a gourd vine to grow near by
To shade the big baby while he had his cry.
But Jonah was angry and dissatisfied,
And said, "The people will say I lied;
I told the people the city would fall,
But they repented and God saved them all."
So God prepared a worm that very next day
And it smote the gourd that it withered away.
Then the sun was so hot on old Jonah's head
That he fainted away and wished he was dead.
Then said the Lord, "You had pity on the vine,

But it was not yours, it was only mine,
You never labored or caused it to grow,
You never reaped it, neither did you sow.
Those are my people as well as the Jew,
They are Adam's posterity and so are you.
So when any repent and turn to God,
I'll save them, Jonah, and spare the rod."

God will save the people from every load,
If they will only trust in the Savior's blood;
If they would turn and upon him call,
No person, city or town would fall. [3]

Two Poems of Old Doc Bailey

Seldom performing as a folk poet was Dr. Ralph Bailey, who retired about 1938, having practiced medicine at Gatesville for fifty years. He would, however, put pencil to paper on occasion, and his lawyer friend, "Judge" J. B. Cross, clung to at least two of his performances. Their dates could be anywhere from the 1900s to the 1930s.

Old Doc Bailey once was aroused to speak in verse after a semiregular outing with cronies on Cowhouse Creek. Gatesville being a dry town, a busthead whiskey was brought from Waco. Called "Cooper's Select," it was aged and bottled by Dick Cooper in the back of his own saloon.

After one of those bosky stag-parties, Doc Bailey brought to Judge Cross a poem he had scribbled on note paper. The Judge obliged his friend by typing a few copies, which, presumably the doctor gave to friends. [4] The Judge kept his own copy as long as he lived and put it in a little book about his old companion.

The title, "A Saving Clause," has to do with the last line. Unevenly imitative of a popular versifier, the form consists mainly of four-stress, frequently iambic lines with internal rhyme, alternating with rhyming three-stress lines. In proper form the poem would run to sixteen lines, and not fifteen, as below:

Last nite I drank, filled up my tank
    On different kinds of booze,
This morn at five, I came alive and puked up
    both my shoes,
I heaved and swore, for an hour or more,
    It was a hellish case.
My anus came through, with a gut or two,
    and stopped right in my face,
I've tasted rot from out the pot
    When just a tiny tad, but no such stuff,
however rough, could equal that by gad,
So I'll bid goodbye to all your rye and
    also to SELECT
Of Roses Four I'll drink no more,
    If I can recollect.

The second poem of Old Doc Bailey may be traditional, and not original with him. It functioned at least once as a professional consultation in his medical practice.

As Judge Cross tells it, one Grandpa Jenkins, who had "many lady admirers," called on the doctor, asking for pills to energize his failing prowess. Doc Bailey responded, "I give you this little verse from an ancient Persian poet." The Judge indicates that Doc Bailey recited the poem to his patient and advised a new hobby as the only recourse.[5]

Authorship not attributed, its two joined quatrains consist of rhymed three-stress lines alternating with unrhymed lines of irregular beat. Here, as in most folk verse, form and rhythm are sacrificed to message.

King Solomon and King David were mighty men—
Leading very active lives,
Each had several hundred concubines and
    many, many wives;
But, when old age came creeping on
    with its many many qualms,
Solomon wrote the Proverbs and
David wrote the Psalms.

TEXAS (Foreign Service)

During the winter of 1941–42 two soldier poems circulated in the old Quadrangle offices at Fort Sam Houston. "TEXAS (Foreign Service)" appeared there as a carbon (typed) "flimsy" copy making the rounds. On onionskin paper several copies can be produced by one typing, but not more than five or six.

The anonymous verses seem to belong to the early training period of World War II, before shipment of troops to Europe. The line "Deep in the heart of Texas" may be an allusion to the Bing Crosby hit song of that time. Professedly written by a non-Texan, its content appeals to Texans in the tall-tale tradition of what J. Frank Dobie called "bragging on the worst."

The poet, as the one whose performance follows this one, uses a stanza of four lines, mostly with three stresses each, some with four, the last line rhyming with the middle one. The rhythm of each is syncopated and basically iambic, that in the second poem perhaps more so than in this.

> There was once that I was happy,
> My life was filled with cheer,
> I never had seen TEXAS
> Till the Army sent me here.
>
> I'd heard songs about her beauty,
> Pretty girls and big strong men,
> Rolling plains, majestic mountains,
> Just Heaven from end to end.
>
> The one thing that is certain,
> Of this there's no denying—
> The guy that spread these rumors
> Did a hell of a lot of lying.
>
> Deep in the heart of Texas
> There's sand in all we eat.
> The girls are all bow-legged,
> The men all have flat feet.

That's why they have to send us here—
Out in this damn direction
Out on this lonely desert,
For this damned state's protection.

No longer are we religious,
We drink, we fight, we curse.
No worry here about going to Hell—
It can't be any worse.

Down here the sun is hotter,
Down here the rain is wetter,
THEY think it's the best state,
But there are Forty-seven better.

Still there's no one to blame but me
The Army never forgot it.
I asked for Foreign Service—
And, by God, I got it!

Upon the Wind-swept Mountains

Untitled and also anonymous, this work is the other that
drifted into the office at Fort Sam. Perhaps in line with somebody's personal filing system, the characters #3 were inked at
the top. Because of reference to desert-like mountains and to
Indians, the verses might have originated in some Arizona or
New Mexico soldier camp.

Here is a clear example of the folk poet sounding off his
personal response to an overwhelming social force, echoing a
sentiment shared by a multitude of his fellow draftees. It is a
sentiment of the "Pre–Pearl Harbor" inductee, pressed into
service for one year only (if peace held out), his pay $21.00
per month for the first three. Then it soared to the regular
$30.00. Hence our saying in the Army at that time, "Another
day, another seventy cents." Even the commonplace Depression Era protest uttered against "Wall Street" was a typical
"gripe" of that decade.

The following quatrains consist of three-stress, syncopated lines.

Upon the wind-swept mountains
    And what a helluva spot
Battling a terrific sand storm
    In the spot that God forgot

Into the sage with a rifle
    Down in the ditch with a pick
Doing the work of a Negro
    And too damn tired to kick

Up with the chickens and Indians
    Up where a man gets blue
Up in the top of the mountains
    And a thousand miles from you.

At night the wind keeps howling
    It's more than a man can stand
Hell now, we're not convicts
    We're defenders of our land.

We are living for tomorrow
    Only to see our gals
Hoping when we return
    They're not married to our pals.

We are soldiers of Selective Service
    We earn our meager pay
Guarding the Wall Street Millions
    For only a dollar a day.

No one knows we're living
    And no one gives a damn
Back home we're soon forgotten
    We've been loaned to Uncle Sam.

Only one year we can stand it
    One year from our lives we'll miss
Boys, don't let the Army get you
    And for Christ's sake don't re-enlist.

The John T. Scopes Trial

"The John T. Scopes Trial" was a professionally produced lyric that cropped up forty years later in oral tradition. At the outset it spoke for one generation, in its reconstruction for another.

These lines are recollected from an old, lost gramophone record. The tune is roughly that of "The Battle Cry of Freedom." Recollected in a spirit of urbane satire, the original agreed with its 1924 audience in the justice of John T. Scopes's conviction for illegally teaching evolution in Tennessee. Its present form was put together from two oral sources by attorney Byron Lockhart, Austin, Texas, apparently in the 1960s.[6]

Byron's major informant was his law partner, Frank Brooks. Frank remembered much of the lyric but was hazy about parts of it. Byron resorted then to T. O. Dillard, whom he described as "an old reprobate lawyer around here like myself, who remembered a lot of old country songs." Lines that Frank could not remember were supplied by T. O. Then Byron, hobby guitarist and songster, typed the words and placed them in his ballad book.

Eventually Byron sent me a photocopy, which represents the lines typed on unruled, three-hole, 6-by-1 & 1/2-inch notebook paper. The last two lines, however, are in pencil, followed by a series of dashes that seem to represent an irrevocably lost last line. It appears that these lines improvise to compensate for what could not be remembered. Again the U.S. Mail augmented the duplicating machine in broadening the poet-performer's audience. I had not asked for the poem, never heard of it. Byron sent it because he knew I would enjoy it.

In general, "The John T. Scopes Trial" follows the pattern of Rudyard Kipling's "Gunga Din." The pattern of the original varied in the final stanza, however, leaving the "more" at the end of the third line without a rhyme and a sixth line. I have supplied a final rhyming line, concluding the poem in the spirit in which it was written.

Oh the folks in Tennessee
    Are as faithful as can be
And they know the Bible teaches what is right.

They believe in God above,
    And his great undying love.
And they know they are protected
    By his might.

You may find a new belief,
    It will only bring you grief,
For a house that's built on sand
    Is sure to fall.

And wherever you may turn,
    There is a lesson you will learn,
That the old religion's better,
    After all.

Then to Dayton came a man
    With his new ideas so grand
And he said "We came from
    Monkeys long ago."

But in teaching this belief,
    Mr. Scopes found only grief,
For they would not let
    Their old religion go.

Then the folks throughout the land
    Saw this house was built on sand
And they said we will not listen any more.
    We believe in what is right
    And for that will always fight,
And we'll send Scopes back to where he was before.

In 1986 the subject of this lyric had again become topical. In Texas, the state public-school textbook controversy had affected the nation's schoolbooks in the dispute over the extent to which evolution (and other subjects) may be presented. A Louisiana law giving "creation science" equal time with evolution in public schools was to be tested in the U.S. Supreme Court. In connection, commentators were invoking the spirit of the 1924 "monkey trial."

The Flying Aggie

It had to happen. The Texas Aggie joke passed into folk poetry from its prolific oral tradition. My "The Flying Aggie" is a photocopy of the work handwritten in pencil on legal-size, ruled tablet paper. As the foregoing, it was mailed to me by one of its co-authors, Byron Lockhart, because he wished to share it with a kindred spirit. He said his collaborator was Bob Ogden, a University of Texas engineering graduate, and the two wrote it, said Byron, "sitting around a table, having a few drinks." The four-line stanza is based on a tune they had in mind, "The Frozen Loggers."

The comedy in this folk poem appeals to the firmly entrenched Texas tradition of joking about the alleged stupidity of anybody connected with Texas A&M University, the universally respected agricultural and mechanical institution of that state. Aggies, like Polacks in the upper Midwestern lore, or Yucatanos in Mexico, have become customary butts of "stupid person" jokes. Ludicrously, this "Flying Aggie" of the space age is glorified because of his stupidity.

I opened my newspaper
 In a restaurant nearby
When a lovely, tattooed waitress
 Let out a fearful cry.

I see that you are an Aggie
 And not just some dude from town;
For nobody but an Aggie
 Holds his paper upside down.

My lover was an Aggie
   His heart was brave and pure.
His arms were strong as crow-bars
   From shoveling manure.

He never used a hammer
   To drive a nail, 'tis said;
For just like an Aggie
   He always used his head.

He would not use deodorants;
   He seldom combed his hair
Scorning toilet paper
   He used a prickly pear.

We planned our wedding shortly
   When he'd be out of school.
For best man he had his room mate—
   A sturdy, loyal mule.

But, hiking on the railroad,
   As a train came roaring down,
He heard its piercing whistle,
   And then I saw him frown.

"An Aggie is no sissy,"
   I heard him firmly say.
He snapped to full attention
   And held the right of way.

The crash shook all of Texas;
   It wrecked the train, I fear.
Into perpetual orbit
   It flung my Aggie dear.

Now every night o'er Bryan,
   Across the purple sky,
Blazing like a comet
   They watch my Aggie fly.

So do not mourn my sweetheart,
   Shed no tears for him.
For his spirit will live forever
   At Texas A & M.

   Eulogy to Gordon Kahl,
   C. P., Taxes and Death

In June 1983, the *Odessa American* printed B. Hammond's lines about Gordon Kahl along with his letter to the editor.[7] By that time having developed an interest in folk poetry, I clipped it out for study (and enjoyment). If it has other preservers, I do not know of them.

In these verses Hammond shares his feelings with those engaged more or less in the nationwide "tax revolt" of the 1980s. Many readers in West Texas (including myself) had followed the adventures of Gordon Kahl, because he recently had labored in the oil patch around Crane and Odessa.

Elements in Kahl's story almost make him a folk hero in the group of which he was a part. Having moved from Texas to North Dakota, he was placed on probation for evasion of federal income taxes. In February 1983, two U.S. marshals were shot to death and three others wounded in an attempt to arrest him. In a stolen police car, Kahl eluded officers for weeks, said to be protected by Posse Comitatus (militant tax evaders) and paramilitary sympathizers. About a hundred policemen with an armored vehicle stormed a hideout; no luck. When his wife, son, and others were charged with killing the marshals, Kahl confessed to the murders, indirectly, through a Posse Comitatus spokesman. In Arkansas in June a sheriff was killed in an attempt to arrest the fugitive. The house under attack caught fire, and Gordon Kahl burned to death.

The makings of a folk hero? He was of the common people. He was an individualist oppressed by organized power. He defied authority. Self-sacrificially, he confessed to murder to protect those dear to him. He was supported by a throng of sympathizers. He was as elusive as Robin Hood in Sherwood Forest, or Gregorio Cortez outsmarting hundreds of lawmen in the South Texas brush country. He fought to a martyr's death for what he thought was right.

In his letter Hammond wrote, "His daughter was quoted as saying that he died a hero's death, as did the lawmen." Agree with Gordon Kahl or not, the makings of a folk hero are there.

In the poem, however, Kahl is represented simply as a victim rather than a hero. Within the month of Kahl's death, Hammond wrote, "I wish to submit an eulogy that typifies one of the underlying causes of unrest and dissatisfaction in this God-blessed America." The lines are a compilation of mainly four-beat couplets, parallel in phrasing, like "When the Jack-ass etc." A few lines run to five beats, including both of the concluding couplet. As in many folk poems of protest, the following protest is tempered with humor.

> They taxed his cow, taxed his goat
> Taxed his pants, taxed his coat
> Taxed his chew, taxed his smoke
> They were going to teach him taxes are no joke.
> They taxed his tractor, taxed his mule,
> They were going to teach him taxes are the rule,
> Taxed his oil, taxed his gas,
> Taxed his notes, taxed his cash;
> They taxed him good to let him know
> After taxes he has no dough.
> They taxed his crops, taxed his work,
> Taxed his tie, taxed his shirt,
> They said, "if he hollers" tax him more;
> Tax him till he's good and sore.
> Tax his coffin, tax his grave,
> Tax the sod in which he lays.
> He put these words upon his tomb:
> "Taxes drove me to my doom."
> And even though he's gone he can't relax,
> They'll still be after the Inheritance Tax.

Oh—Good Lord

Suitable for recitation at parties, as a so-called "toast," these couplets were mailed to me in the 1970s, handwritten in ink on ruled notebook paper, with the notation "origin unknown" at the bottom. They came from James A. Neale, retired from Civil Service in Wichita Falls, Texas. Folklore studies had nothing to do in his sharing with me these lines, which he knew would give me a chuckle.

Almost unique in folk poetry is the unconventional subtlety in the title. It does not tell what the poem is about, a practice not uncommon among literary poets. In one sense the title praises the Lord for endowing man with longevity connected with an appetite for booze. In another, more far-fetched, sense, it is a common utterance of surprised reaction to the humorous or trivial, in this case the poem itself.

In this group of one-sentence couplets, the lines adhere to the four-stress iambic rhythm with regularity uncommon in folk poetry. There will be seen, however, a few exceptions.

> The horse and mule live thirty years,
> Yet know nothing of wines and beers.
>
> Most goats and sheep at twenty die,
> And have never tasted Scotch or Rye.
>
> A cow drinks water by the ton,
> So at eighteen is mostly done.
>
> A dog in milk and water soaks,
> And then in twelve short years he croaks.
>
> Your modest, sober, bone-dry hen
> Lays eggs for Nogs, then dies at ten.
>
> All animals are strickly dry,
> They sinless live and swiftly die.
>
> But sinful, ginful, beer soaked men,
> Survives three score years and ten.
>
> While some of us, though mighty few,
> Stay sozzled till we're ninety two.

Untitled Courtroom Limericks

One of the most-often practiced conventional forms in folk poetry is that of the limerick. Both oral and printed tradition swell with it. These three might not be immortal, but they were considered newsworthy in 1984 by an Associated Press reporter. Printed all over the country, they came to my attention in the *Odessa American*.[8]

During a Phoenix, Arizona, murder trial, the contending lawyers wrote limericks to each other. They speak of the agreement reached by the prosecutor and defense counsel to drop the case. Hence, folk poetry arising as a whimsical expression of the poet's occupation.

A man named White was on trial for pumping five bullets into his housemate, whose first name was Frank and who seems to have been a motorcyclist. Frank, whose autopsy indicated that he died drunk, broke down the door to White's room and was shot as an unknown intruder. In view of the circumstances, the prosecutor decided to "dump" the case, that is, drop the charge against White.

This action prompted the defense to dash off a limerick and pass it on to the prosecutor. It read:

> There once was a man named White,
> Whose roommate wanted to fight.
>   White was charged with a crime
>   And could have done time.
> Cleve dumped it 'cause it wasn't right.

His lyric prowess stirred, Cleve replied to Defense Counsel Logan:

> There was an attorney named Logan,
> Whose skill as a poet was token.
>   His client named White
>   Barred the door in the night
> And shot when the door jamb was broken.

Logan replied with two limericks, only one of which went into the Associated Press story. It read:

There once was a biker named Frank
Who got violent whenever he drank.
    His blood was 2-4
    When he crashed through White's door.
Cleve dumped it, he knew it was rank.

Why his story did not include the fourth limerick, the reporter saith not. All four were entered into the trial record by the judge and are open to inspection in the Phoenix District Clerk's office.

Ode to the Seat Belt

These lines appeared in the "Messages from Mars" column of editor Marlea Crittenden in a *Moody Courier* of 1985. She says they were written by the Director of the University of Texas at Arlington News Service and were sent to her by mail.

Here is a folk poem that chooses sides, after presenting both, on a controversial social issue universally shared in Texas. When the author wrote these lines, all Texas was abuzz at the new state seat belt law: Buckle up or get fined. Radio talk-shows and letters to editors crackled with protests against this violation of a person's right to run any deadly risk he chooses. There were, of course, defenders of the measure. Though this poem complains of the inconvenience, even embarrassment, of using the belt, common sense prevails.

The conventional four-line stanzas that follow are more careful to speak plainly than to confine the rhythm to a predominant regular pattern.

I've buckled up for safety;
I'm complying with the law
Though my blouses are wrinkled
And my neck has been rubbed raw.

Got a strap across my belly
But what sticks inside my craw
Is the one across my chest
That fits like a too-tight bra.

I can't even reach the glove box
To retrieve a simple map
Without filling up my mouth
With a lousy two-inch strap

When I try to order Big Macs
This is how it goes:
I have to fight the belt
'Cause it's cutting off my nose.

I feel like I'm a chauffeur
Cause friends hate the belts, you see
And when we go to lunch
They won't ride up front with me.

But what really makes me mad
Are the grins and all the stares
From the bozos watchin' me
Who, bygum, ain't wearin' their's!

Some say they never will
Wear that vinyl sash
But they can blame themselves
When their face lies on the dash.

Too bad we have to legislate
What's just for our own good
But I'd rather have a wrinkled shirt
Than go through the window to the hood. [9]

The Noche Before Christmas

Much of Texas is strongly biethnic, resulting in a sprinkling of English talk with Spanish, and Spanish with English. An Anglo will say, "Let's go to the baile [dance]." I heard a

Mexican-American say to another, "Ella cree you bandido" [She thought you were a bandit]. Somehow italics seem inappropriate to expressions like these in print.

Such a folk poem in both oral and print tradition is the parody, "The Noche before Christmas." Essentially in English, it assumes a smattering of Spanish in its audience and uses it for humorous effect. Because of its oral transmission, there are at least three variants. I have heard parts of it recited by a few individuals, always about Christmas time. Those parts stressed the calamity awaiting Papa on Christmas Eve when he encounters Mama. It observes—and departs from—both content and form of the well-known "Visit from St. Nicholas" by Clement C. Moore.

The version printed in 1982 in *Amigos*, an El Paso newspaper for tourists, goes like this:

> 'Twas the night before Christmas
>   And all through the casa,
> Not a creature was stirring.
>   Caramba! Que pasa?
>
> The stockings were hung
>   Con mucho cuidado,
> In hopes that Saint Nicholas
>   Would feel obligado
>
> To leave some cositas
>   Aqui and alli,
> For niño and niña
>   And something for me.
>
> The children were snuggled
>   All safe in their camas
> Some in vestidos
>   And some in pyjamas.
>
> Chihuahua! Que esta?
>   Es Santa Claus gordo,
> Con sleigh muy chiquita,
>   And ocho venados.

Pancho and Pedro,
　　And Comet and Vixen,
Rodolfo, Ernesto,
　　And Donner and Blitzen.

And leaving regalos
　　And dulces and frutas,
Santa waves his fat arms,
　　Crying "Muchos saludos,

Adios, Buenos Noches,
　　Merry Christmas," he calls,
"Feliz Navidad, and
　　Happy New Year to all." [10]

Then the *Amigos* writer observed that "as stories go from person to person they are changed." He proceeded to present two variants, both of which substitute for the last three stanzas of the foregoing. The form altered by oral transmission, the four-line stanza no longer quite applies. To be noted is the bilingual coinage "zigzagando." The first variant says:

Their cabezas are full of good things
They're all esperando que Santa will bring.

Santa esta at the corner saloon,
Muy boracho since midafternoon.
Mama is sitting beside la ventana,
Shining her rolling pin para mañana,
When Santa returns home zigzagando
Lit up like the Star Spangled banner, cantando.
Mama will send him to bed con a right:
Merry Christmas a todos y a todos: Good night! [11]

The form of the second variant departs even further from Moore's than the first.

Mama is sitting beside la ventana,
But Santa will come
En un manner extrano

Lit up like the star
On the mountain, cantando
Y mama le manda
To bed with a right.
Merry Christmas a todos,
Y a todos, Good Night.[12]

Resembling their literary counterparts, folk poems attain a modest life of their own. Each, in its own limited world, is circulated, and perhaps treasured by the few who like it for what it says and the way it says it. Usually the folk poem is as ephemeral as a scrap of paper or a garrulous whim. It might, however, live briefly in print, to be preserved by burial in a moldering newspaper file. By slim chance, it might enjoy serendipitous resurrection. It might circulate briefly in copies by hand or machine, only to die with a batch of personal papers in a trash can. Even so, it might be discovered and given a new start. While skillful form is not vital to a folk poem, a touch of humor seems to be an elixir for most. All that keeps some of these performances barely alive is their simple appeal to kindred spirits who copy and share.

Notes

For discussions of folk poetry, see T. M. Pearce, "What Is a Folk Poet?" *Western Folklore* 12 (1953): 242–48; Américo Paredes, "Some Aspects of Folk Poetry," *Texas Studies in Literature and Language* 6 (1964): 213–25; and James McNutt, "Cowboy Poetry," *Texas Heritage*, Spring 1985, pp. 8–11.

1. It would be easy—but not very—to explain how most lines of these folk poems are mixtures of various metrical feet with their Greek names. This is to say nothing of syllables absent or added at the beginning or end of a line. The lines, then, are described simply as "syncopated," in contrast with the well-known, regular iambic line, "The proper study of mankind is man."
2. *The Pioneer News Observer* (San Angelo, Tex.), 14 August 1974,

reprinted from the *Dodge City* (Kans.) *Ford County Globe,* 27 August 1878.

3. *Coryell County News* (Gatesville, Tex.), 2 June 1933.
4. Judge R. B. Cross, *Tales of Old Doc Bailey* (Waco, Tex.: Davis Bros. Publishing Co., 1965), pp. 1–2.
5. Cross, *Tales of Old Doc Bailey,* pp. 18–19.
6. Byron Lockhart, Austin, Texas, telephone interview, 23 August 1986.
7. "Letters," *Odessa* (Tex.) *American,* 20 June 1983, reprinted by permission of the publisher.
8. "There Were Two Poets in Phoenix," *Odessa* (Tex.) *American,* 5 August 1984, reprinted by permission of the publisher.
9. "Messages from Mars," *Moody* (Tex.) *Courier,* 17 October 1985.
10. *El Paso* (Tex.) *Amigos,* 15 December 1982.
11. Ibid.
12. Ibid.

For additional folk poems in English, see Elton Miles, *More Tales of the Big Bend,* to be published in 1988 by the Texas A&M University Press. The collection includes "The Pecos River Queen," "You Must Not Trot My Cows, Boys," "Ranger Life," "The Drilling Man," "The Sheriff's Job," and "Ode to Doctors on Call." The poems were written by ranchwomen, housewives, cowboys, an oil patch roughneck, and lawmen.

CONTRIBUTORS

MRS. JOHN Q. ANDERSON, now of Ruston, Louisiana, was a resident of Austin, College Station, and Houston during her twenty-three-year residence in Texas. She has been a public school teacher, newspaper editor, journalist, and compiler of several genealogical works. She designed and compiled the *Index to Studies in Philology: Vols. I–L.* Loraine is a regular contributor to TFS programs.

LAWRENCE CLAYTON is presently Dean of the College of Arts and Sciences and Professor of English at Hardin-Simmons University in Abilene, Texas. His principal interest is in the folklore, folk life, and literature of the American West with emphasis on contemporary materials. His most recent publications include *Clear Fork Cowboys* (with photographs by Sonja Irwin Clayton)—a study of cowboy culture along the Clear Fork of the Brazos River—and *Elmer Kelton,* in the Boise State University Western Writers Series. In addition, he has edited *"There's Always Another Chance" and Other Stories*—a collection of the pulp stories of fiction writer Elmer Kelton. He has published in earlier collections of the Society, as well as in such journals as *Western Folklore, Southern Folklore Quarterly, Folklore Forum, Western American Literature,* and *Southwestern American Literature.*

KENNETH W. DAVIS is a graduate of Texas Tech and Vanderbilt. He teaches American Folklore at Texas Tech, where he is a professor of English. A native Texan, he is much interested in oral narratives of Texas and the Southwest.

LORA B. GARRISON is a traditional storyteller, sixth-generation Texan, and a descendant of ranchers, preachers, and shinglemakers. A long-time area historian, she collects oral histories of early settlers of the Texas Hill Country. She is a regular contributor to the Barker Texas History Library, is recognized by local, regional, and state institutions for her preservation of the Hill Country heritage, and she writes a column called "Stomping Grounds" for the *Uvalde Leader News*.

JOE S. GRAHAM of Millican is Professor of English at Texas A&M. He was born and raised in the Big Bend and is a long-time and invaluable contributor to the Society and all of its activities.

JIM HARRIS attended colleges in Nacogdoches and Commerce, Texas, and taught in Louisiana and Texas before moving to Hobbs, New Mexico, where he lives with his wife Mary and son Hawk. He teaches English at New Mexico Junior College, edits *Southwestern American Literature* with John O. West, publishes small books through his Hawk Press, and walks the deserts and forests of his adopted state.

GUY LOGSDON, University of Tulsa, has collected and written for many years about Southwestern folklore and personalities including cowboy songs and poetry, Bob and Johnnie Lee Wills and western swing, Woody Guthrie, Hopalong Cassidy, and other personalities and topics. In 1982 he was the Oklahoma coordinator for the Smithsonian Institution's Annual Festival of Folklife with Oklahoma as the featured state. He has produced over twenty television shows about Southwestern folklife and has been a consultant for movies and television. Logsdon is presently revising his manuscript of "ugly" cowboy songs and co-producing a documentary about western swing.

AL LOWMAN of Stringtown is on the staff of the Institute of Texan Cultures in San Antonio. His long-time interest in the history, folklore, and art of the Southwest has resulted in several books, the latest of which is *Remembering Carl Hertzog, A Texas Printer and His Books*.

ELTON MILES is Professor Emeritus of English at Sul Ross State University, Alpine, Texas, where he taught for thirty-two years. He is still collecting folklore of the Big Bend. Several of his pieces have appeared in publications of the Texas Folklore Society, of which he is a past president. Two of his books are *The Way I Heard It* and *Tales of the Big Bend*. Another, *More Tales of the Big Bend*, should appear in 1988.

CHARLIE ODEN retired from the Espee in 1981 after forty-plus years with Southern Pacific's Dallas and San Antonio divisions. He presently maintains a part-time tax practice, serves on the Board of Directors of the Houston Folklore Society, writes for *The Crosstie*, the San Antonio Division magazine/newsletter, and is a member of the Texas Folklore Society, Canadian Folk Music Society, Austin Writers' League, 36th Infantry Division Association, and the Houston Audubon Society.

PALMER OLSEN is the Society's venerable member from Bosque County. His biography precedes his article.

PAUL PATTERSON of Crane, a far-west Texan by birth and preference, has ridden and written about that area for three-fourths of a hundred years and does not intend to change ranges or subjects.

JOYCE GIBSON ROACH of Keller, Texas, is a prolific writer, winner of the America Spur award for *The Cowgirls*, producer of the musical *Texanna* for the Sesquicentennial, teacher, lecturer, musician—and a High Toned Woman.

EDWARD C. ROWLAND has served on the Board of the Texas Association of Museums, has been Director of the Big Thicket Museum and the Fort Jackson U.S. Army Museum in South Carolina, and is now the Executive Vice President and Director of the Petroleum Museum, Library, and Hall of Fame in Midland, Texas.

ERNEST B. SPECK of Alpine is a native of Llano County. He left the worn-out, sandy-land cotton patches to become a college English teacher. Ernest edited *Mody Boatright, Folklorist* in 1973 and is Mody's literary executor. Now retired, he continues to write about farm folklore.

JACK WELCH has documented baptistry paintings since 1977 and has published articles on Appalachian baptistry paintings. Welch is a professor of English at Abilene Christian University, where he teaches composition, creative writing, and Christian fiction. Welch's new novel, *Feeling Free,* is due out in summer, 1987.

JOHN O. WEST joined the TFS in 1961 and has served the Society as Councillor, Vice-President, President, Trustee, and has helped write more annual resolutions than most folks would like to remember. Articles by John O. have appeared in about half a dozen annuals, and well over a dozen papers—chiefly on Mexican-American folklore—by this West Texan have disturbed the peace of the annual meetings. He founded *The American Folklore Newsletter* and edited it (with wife Lucy) for its first seven years. He teaches English and Folklore at the University of Texas at El Paso.

INDEX

The Texas Folklore Society Series

Other TFS annual publications available from SMU Press are listed below:

XXIX.   *And Horns on the Toads* (1959). Boatright, Hudson, and Maxwell, eds.
XXX.   *Singers and Storytellers* (1961). Boatright, Hudson, and Maxwell, eds.
XXXI.   *The Golden Log* (1962). Boatright, Hudson, and Maxwell, eds.
XXXII.   *A Good Tale and a Bonnie Tune* (1964). Boatright, Hudson, and Maxwell, eds.
XXXIII.   *The Sunny Slopes of Long Ago* (1966). Hudson and Maxwell, eds.
XLV.   *Folk Art in Texas* (1985). Abernethy, ed.
XLVI.   *Sonovagun Stew* (1986). Abernethy, ed.
An *Analytical Index to Publications of the Texas Folklore Society, Volumes 1–36* (1973) is also available.